WHY ME? WHY NOW? WHY NOT?

Finding Opportunity In Your Obstacles

by Trish Whynot

For further information, please contact Trish Whynot, 10 Maple Street, Suite 100, Middleton, Massachusetts 01949.

Editor: Bree Ervin
Proofreader: Brigitta Patterson
Cover design: Jeff Maust
Book design: Brian Schwartz

ISBNs:

978-0-9883377-0-1 (Print)
978-0-9883377-1-8 (ePub)

Table of Contents

Dedication

Why Me? Why Now? Why Not? is dedicated to those who are ready to delve deeper and soar higher.

Acknowledgments

I acknowledge with delight and humility:

Family, friends, clients, students, teachers, pets and even acquaintances who have inspired me to seek for Love just by being themselves and living life as best they knew how. I hope my graceful as well as my awkward moments have inspired them similarly.

Foreword

While the book you are about to read is quite manageable in terms of page count, it is generously massive in terms of wisdom. In fact, this book is entirely reflective of the author's approach to counseling, which is to cut through to the heart of any issue and heal it using the most profound-yet-economical processes.

Every time I read Dr. Trish Whynot's writing, I'm taken aback by "her ability to see through the chaos of life's web and identify the root cause of any problem." That's a quotation from an article I wrote about Trish more than 12 years ago, and it's still the essence of her work from my perspective. She has the natural ability to see past the smokescreen of drama, chaos and emotion and recognize the true origin of our physical, mental, social and even financial issues. Once identified, healing those issues is pretty straightforward, although not necessarily easy. According to Trish, the "easy" depends upon your willingness to accept responsibility for your life and then your willingness to allow it to change.

Accepting responsibility for our life is a big part of Trish's work. In her counseling and in this book, she pinpoints exactly how to own the responsibility of our problems—removing blame and victimhood from the equation—so that we are empowered to actually create change. This is critically important considering that we have no power to change others. So waiting for others to change before we can be healthy, happy or successful can be a long, arduous wait. Instead, Trish provides a gentle and loving approach that allows us to accept responsibility for our circumstances and then move beyond them with joy and inner peace. And this can all be done with remarkable swiftness.

I first became aware of Dr. Trish Whynot in the year 2000 when I interviewed her for an article I was writing for OfSpirit.com Magazine, where I'm the editor. She absolutely blew my mind during that interview, so much that I began seeing her for transformative therapy myself and have recommended her to my audience, my family members and my friends ever since. Just this month, now twelve years since I first met her, I referred another friend to Trish.

I had a significant, spiritual awakening that took place around the time that I first met Trish, and the paradigm shift that I gained from what she taught me was instrumental in this awakening. What she taught me is what she teaches in this book, and I'll mention just a small sample here:

- Our life circumstances, our relationships and our

bodies are trying to teach us something; that is, our illnesses, accidents, coincidences, social interactions and even our pets are attempting to guide us toward the experiences we came into this life to comprehend.

- Every day is a new opportunity to create change in our lives. And with the proper awareness, we can either glide with the flow of life or struggle against its current.

- Our ability to forgive, which is as important for our own inner peace as it is for those we forgive, is one of our greatest challenges. And the depth of rewards that come from forgiving is in direct relation to the level of difficulty it is to forgive.

- At the root of everything is our relationship with our selves and our relationship with Source (God, Creative Intelligence, the Universe).

- A spiritual approach to any pursuit—including weight loss, making money or sports—always brings us to a deeper perspective.

- When we are ready to own our choices and the results of those choices, we are ready to transform our lives with increased love, joy and compassion.

I'll give you an example that I like to share when telling

people about my past experiences with Trish. I went to see her in my late 30s because I noticed that whenever I saved some money, some event would occur (sometimes a series of events) that quickly depleted my savings. My car would break down. My dog or cat had to visit the emergency room (where fees were a lot more expensive than at their normal veterinarian office). Or I had to pay taxes or buy a new computer or something of that nature. Whatever it was that happened, the end result was always the same—before I knew it, I no longer had any savings.

In my work with Trish to understand this recurring experience, I recognized that I was repeating a pattern that I'd learned in my youth. I discovered this when Trish had me meditate with the intention of recalling events throughout my life when this issue first appeared. In this meditation, I saw myself at three different ages as a boy having experiences that created this undesirable pattern.

At the earliest age, around twelve, my father took me to the racetrack. I was always pretty lucky at winning things and that night I won $150, which I put into my piggy bank. A short time later, my parents borrowed that money in order to pay some bills; and because they were never able to get ahead financially, they were never able to return it. At a later age, around fourteen, I sold my drum set in order to buy a better one. But before buying the new drum set, my parents borrowed the money to pay some bills and, again, were unable to ever return it. In the third memory, which took place around the age of sixteen, I sold my motorcycle. And, again, in the weeks that followed, my parents had to borrow the money and were never able to return it.

Following the meditation, Trish helped me to process these memories, specifically this recurring pattern that had been created around money in my youth. She taught me to understand how my anticipation of that recurring outcome (that saved money disappears) could lead me to recreate that in my adult life. If you understand the law of attraction and how we attract what we expect from life, it makes perfect sense that I could manifest these events that depleted my savings whenever I began to get ahead financially. And bringing this realization to my awareness was all I needed to interrupt the pattern. From that day forward, I have been able to save money with ease.

But Trish didn't stop there. She taught me how to heal this issue at a much deeper level, which meant making sure that I didn't feel negativity toward my parents for what happened and making sure that I didn't feel victimized by their actions. She aided me in understanding the financial struggle my parents had while raising my sister and I, yet without ever making us feel their plight. My father was a truck driver and my mother stayed home to raise us kids. And because money for rent and utilities was often tight, my parents had to meet their financial demands with whatever was within their reach. And sometimes that meant borrowing money from their kids. How were they to know what subconscious lessons they were teaching by not having the means to pay us back?

In the end, Trish walked me through some steps to have compassion for my parents who were just trying to provide our family with the best life they knew how to provide. Trish reminded me that it was my soul who chose these two people as my parents in order to provide the early experiences I intended to have in life. And this was my opportunity to forgive my parents for these three experiences around money that I had as a boy. Taking it one step further, this allowed me to feel gratitude for the lessons this issue taught me as an adult, especially the valuable lesson about the power of our mind to create life as we expect it. In the end, my work with Trish not only ended my life-long pattern of not being able to save money, it also taught me to feel a newfound compassion, gratitude and love for my mother and father.

I've only touched upon a small fragment of the wisdom this book offers, because the potential it holds to improve your relationships, your career, your health and, yes, your happiness is exceptionally difficult to communicate. Yet Trish has an extraordinary knack for explaining complicated subjects and making them easy to understand. Better yet, she's provided case studies—real stories with actual clients— that spell out exactly how we can apply the lessons that she's teaching.

I love books like this that lend themselves to reading from the first chapter to the last OR reading chapters in random order without losing any comprehension. This is one of those books that allows you to pick it up, choose a random chapter, and see what lessons are in store for you. If you trust in this process, more often than not you'll pick a chapter that is exactly what you need to be reading at that moment.

If what you read in this book resonates with you and you want to take your personal growth to a higher level, I highly recommend working with Trish one-on-one. Since she can just as easily work with you by phone as she can in person, private sessions are the perfect way to apply the brilliance of Trish's philosophies to your individual life and situations. But begin by reading this book first, because you might be one of those people who instantly grasps Trish's way of thinking and can apply it to your life without assistance. If so, you are going to see your life improving in new directions that you might never have considered. I know I've had a great deal of growth that I can directly attribute to what I've learned from Trish. And I'm thrilled that she has now written this book in order to share her wisdom in this way.

Bob Olson
OfSpirit.com editor
Kennebunkport, Maine
September 2012

"Why me?" "Why this?" "Why now?"
"Why not?"

Intro

As a child I frequently found myself asking "Why not?" The most popular response inevitably fell into some version of "Because I said so."

Sound familiar?

That answer was never very satisfying to my inquisitive mind.

Eventually I even married someone with this last name. For real. How does that happen? Unrelenting curiosity and a refusal to take "Because I said so" for an answer?

When a doctor told me that I would just have to live with sinus problems I silently responded on the way out of his office, "I don't think so." Fortunately, as a result of still being adverse to "Because I said so," this diagnosis sent me searching for answers rather than into resignation.

The medical community was telling me that I couldn't overcome my chronic condition and I wanted to know, "Why not?" The answers that have brought relief to my physical, social and financial discord have been my God-honest

responses to questions such as, "Why me?" "Why this?"
"Why now?" "Why not?" This yearning to understand life's
offerings even led to a career-change from the field of
business to that of holistic counselor but my studies didn't
end there.

"The only source of knowledge is experience." ~ Albert
Einstein[1]

I used to be one of those people who would be quick to
tell you that something didn't bother me when deep down
inside it did. That was how I had learned to cope. I was even
proud of how I had mastered this version of pridefulness.
But it was this dishonest methodology that led to my health
problems, relationship discord and financial challenges.

We are in a relationship with everything—with people,
with our health, and even with our finances. Experience is
our teacher. When the fruit of our labors is health,
relationship or financial discord, it is a heads-up that we may
have encountered an insane coping skill such as
pridefulness. Insane, because it is incapable of providing us
with the results our hearts are seeking.

"You cannot evaluate an insane belief system from within
it," states the Foundation for Inner Peace's edition of *A
Course in Miracles*.

Being prideful is like riding the bike to nowhere. As with

a stationary bike, it provides us with exercise (things to do) but it doesn't provide us with the nutrients (scenery) from which our spirits can thrive.

Humility was and still is my antidote for pridefulness—humility as the openness and willingness to embrace what is, not as an end in itself, but as a pathway toward something extraordinary.

This book is my attempt to describe what I have learned from life's challenges—how discomfort, when it shows up, can be successfully utilized as a springboard to living more, loving more and being more. The language used is a mixture of personal growth and spirituality (not religious) because both pursuits, when authentic, are paths of Truth and Love. One is from the inside-out and the other is from the outside-in. Based on my experience, no matter where you begin, if you follow it far enough, one leads to the other. Spirituality is your personal relationship with Something More. Call it what you will—be it Universal Intelligence, Life Force, Quantum Physics or God. I used my terms of endearment, but please feel free to substitute your terms for Truth and Love for your optimal understanding.

Not much else is working these days. The population has never been more medicated, obesity is rampant, our economy is collapsing and the news is overflowing with victim stories.

So why not focus on what we do have the power to change for a change?

Why not help the medical community, our economy and our interpersonal relationships by giving blaming, victimhood and resignation a rest and focusing on how we may be unknowingly contributing to our own discord?

Why me? Why now? Why not?

The information to follow has the potential to:

- bring light to your confusion.

- bring order to your chaos.

- be a powerful adjunct to mainstream and alternative healing treatments.

- inspire your own fresh perspectives.

- help you discern between what is serving and what is sabotaging you.

- reveal how your spiritual and everyday lives are interwoven.

- disclose the secret(s) that will eliminate the root of your problem(s).

In order to be sure that something no longer fits who I am, I have to try it on at least one last time.

Chapter 1
Seeds of Change: Transitions in Mothering

My husband has been after me to do something with the seeds in our catchall drawer. "I'm going to plant them in the spring." has been my response for the last few years. But springs have come and gone and the only growth that appears to be happening is that of the size of the pile of seeds in the drawer.

I have an affection for gardening. I even dried these seeds myself. Hence, my lack of follow through with planting is a sign of change for me. It is a hint that I have outgrown this activity—outgrown it because it doesn't fit who I am anymore.

In order to be sure that something no longer fits who I am, I have to try it on at least one last time. So this past year I planted some seeds. I have always tended to seeds with the caring heart of a new mother, but this time it felt more like a chore. My heart wasn't in it.

My life has changed dramatically over the past few years.

My youngest graduated from college and the older two have married. These changes had an affect on all aspects of my maternal nature.

My affection for gardening has not diminished, but adopting from the nursery has been more appealing during my transition out of motherhood. Tending to plants that others have lovingly germinated brings me joy now. I take great pleasure in my new freedom.

So what about the seeds in my drawer—the physical remnants of my motherhood? They are truly seeds of change. My lessons from motherhood are within me. The joy of their memories remains deep within my heart.

It is easy to picture myself without young children of my own these days, but gardenless? My garden continues to reflect the changes in my life, and the joy of planting seeds could return with the coming of grandchildren. But for now giving the job to someone who enjoys it as much as I used to makes the most sense.

I revere my relationships with everything in my life, including the seeds in my drawer, so when something stops bringing me joy it deserves some reflection. Sometimes a relationship is ready to be redefined or changed in some way and sometimes it is time for the activity to be passed along to someone new or for the activity to be retired.

Just tossing something so poignant into the trash seemed disrespectful. But celebrating the closure of my germinating days with gratitude and a little ritual would honor my liberation and express my appreciation for Mother Nature's role in my life.

The woods near our home provided the perfect environment for returning the aging seeds to their Great Mother. I expressed my gratitude for all the healing, rejuvenating and growth those germinating days had provided. Mother Nature had, indeed, been by my side for the entire journey, even during times when I was unaware of Her presence.

I look forward to discovering new ways of connecting, enjoying and seeking Her counsel. My future adventures are likely to provide us with lots of new material.

Why me? Why now? Why not?

Questions to inspire your own healthy transition:

- *Is there an item or activity that no longer fits who you are?*

- *How did it serve you?*

- *How can you set it free with reverence? (Re-gift, re-purpose or retire with gratitude and appreciation.)*

God tucks away truths about love in memories from our childhood. Redeeming these truths transforms us from victim to visionary.

Chapter 2
A Tale of Two Dads: Truths About Love

Annalee was a month shy of seven and learning to ride a two-wheeler on the street where Uncle James lived. "I should already be riding a two-wheeler." Annalee was thinking. All her friends were. She had been begging her dad to teach her for months.

This day was actually her uncle's idea. Taylor Street was flat and Annalee lived on a hill so it made sense to learn here. Uncle James was there with his daughter, Peggy, and Anna was with her dad. Annalee was six months older than Peggy, a year older in school, and a head taller.

Peggy was already mastering the whole bike thing, but Annalee was struggling. "My bike is too big for me." Anna pouted. Her parents had bought her one that she would grow into, but that didn't help her at all with her learning. Peggy's bike was just her size, just what she needed.

Annalee secretly wished that Uncle James were her dad. There were many days that this secret wish haunted her. Uncle James was a cool dad. He did things with his kids. You could tell that he really enjoyed them and he enjoyed Annalee. She could feel it in her heart.

After another failed attempt at riding, disgusted with her dad and fuming at God, Anna silently demanded of Him, "Why me? What did I do to deserve this dad?" It felt as though her dad was always wishing she'd hurry and grow up already, as the bigger bike implied. Annalee wasn't having fun or feeling enjoyed, but Dad put on a good show that day on Taylor Street just as he always did.

Forty years later Annalee recounts this memory and sees the contrast between authentic love and synthetic love. Authentic love is like a beam of light that comes from within and radiates outward, warming the hearts of those in its path. Uncle James had loved her authentically, enjoyed his time with her and warmed her with his glow.

There was no warmth from her own dad on that day. There was no authentic love that accompanied doing a fatherly duty to uphold a fatherly image because it was a pursuit to be in the spotlight rather than the source of the beam. That was synthetic love—it looked like love but it didn't feel like love.

In reality, God had gifted Annalee with a great truth. She just didn't have the maturity to understand it at the time, so it was ingeniously sandwiched into a memory that could serve her later. " I guess I owe God an apology."

acknowledged Annalee as she redeemed this timely wisdom and promptly applied it to her currently synthetic circumstances. Finding herself in her dad's shoes was humbling to say the least.

Why me? Why now? Why not?

Questions to inspire your own reawakening:

- *Is there a memory from your childhood that is ready for revisiting?*

- *What was your interpretation then?*

- *How might it be of value to your living more, loving more or being more today?*

Truth without love is condescending, and love without truth is enabling. But truth with love is liberating.

Chapter 3
Is It Loving Or Is It Selfish?
How Fear Taints Love

I thought the difference between being loving and being selfish was obvious. Aren't they opposites? Well, they may actually be the opposite of what you think. Learned behaviors and beliefs about love modeled during childhood become our love habits as adults, so what you have been practicing may warrant a second glance.

When I laid my beliefs out on the table for reevaluation, some of them made no sense. Some of what I was practicing as love created frustration for me.

How could love create frustration?

I didn't think it could, so I dedicated a period of time to reevaluating and redefining my definition of love. If peace of mind, integrity and authenticity are virtues you seek, I urge you to undertake such a reevaluation yourself.

We all enter this world with a longing to love and be loved; the means to this end is where it gets confusing. Genuinely loving thoughts, words and deeds, must come from a place that is pure-of-heart. Pure-of-heart as in absent-of-fear. It takes openness, brutal honesty and a willingness to consume lots of humble pie in order to distinguish what is loving from what is selfishness.

Giving the Shirt Off One's Back

Some religions and societies profess that it is noble and saintly, indeed loving, to put one's self last. In an effort to mimic saints who came from a loving place that was pure-of-heart, many have misguidedly resorted to manipulative and controlling tactics with selfish motives. Actions that can appear honorable and noble on the surface can conceal fear-based intentions beneath. When the intentions match the actions it is love. "As above, so below" you might say.

When someone asks a favor of us and we comply, even though we are already spread too thin, what we feel is not aligned with what we do. "As above is not so below."

Would you want to be on the receiving end of someone's help if you knew it meant that they had to suffer to be there for you?

Probably not. Suffering doesn't prove that someone loves us. And it isn't even necessary.

Suffering more likely indicates:

- a fear of the consequences of saying "no."

- a desire to monopolize the attention, admiration or sympathy of those they profess to be helping.

- an inflated sense of self-importance—a false belief that they are indispensable.

- a lack of faith and trust that there is someone else who will step up in their absence.

These kinds of behaviors are actually selfish because they are born of fear and block out divine intervention.

The selfish-of-heart have a strong desire to love and be loved, but have been misguided. They don't understand the process and can be destructive and even arrogant in their refusal to own their motivations. You can give someone the shirt off your back as long as it doesn't cause harm anywhere else.

If you will freeze or have to ask someone else for their shirt, are you really helping anyone?

Fear-Based Motivations

Fear-based motivations promote intentions that are selfish rather than loving. They include fear of not being loved for being honest, fear of what others will think and fear of going to hell. Ironically, when selfish-of-heart we expend a lot more energy in our attempts to get others to believe that we are pure-of-heart, than those who are pure-of-heart spend on being loving.

When fearful we manipulate. We try to earn love rather than express love; we attempt to prove that we love rather than trust in the power of love. When tactics fail to produce a desired outcome it leaves us frustrated. Authentic love does not create frustration, so when we find ourselves frustrated because someone does not appreciate our loving efforts, it is likely we were manipulating rather than loving.

When pure-of-heart we have nothing to prove, nothing to hide, and no need to defend or justify, only a desire to love and be honest.

The Pure-Of-Heart Don't Take, They Attract

Messengers for the Divine, such as Christ and Buddha, were pure-of-heart. They were living examples of their teachings: inspiring us and showing us our potential just by being themselves. The attractiveness of their pure intentions, loving expressions, and the fruit of their labors inspired loving.

Lost in their need to control, many modern-day role models and authority figures have forgotten the true source of their power—the power of love. We can't teach with authority what we aren't practicing. Those who are fear-based practice control and domination over others, call it power and teach it as such. When we desire to develop our God-given power, our power to love and be loved, we will attract a teacher on the pure-of-heart path.

To love authentically involves taking responsibility for any limitations between our hearts and our desires. When there is no resistance to a desire it fulfills itself instantaneously. Expressing to someone that our motives are rooted in anger or fear, even if in the moment we don't know why, can be more loving than pretending that everything is just fine. Unexpressed emotions can spill over and hurt others. This is one reason why it is important to express our feelings—not for the purpose of justifying or excusing our behavior, or to blame others, but for the purpose of loving and healing. Denying feelings to appear the better person or to avoid conflict is selfish and hurtful.

A Friend in Need May Not be a Friend Indeed

If we are too busy to be there for someone when their life is going well, but would be there in a heartbeat if they were in crisis, our motives may be worth reexamining.

Would you want a person like that near you during a time of need?

The selfish want to be there for us if they can benefit in some way, so an opportunity to be a hero is enticing. When we are feeling undervalued we are in need, so it would be more loving to address our own issues than to go on a *help* mission to feed our lack of self-worth with someone else's misfortune. People sometimes use their misfortune to get attention. That is selfish too.

Compassion and pity are two very different motivators. Those who have used a crisis to positively change the course of their lives look back with gratitude. So when someone comes into my office feeling like their world is falling apart, I feel for them, but I don't feel bad for them, because I know that they are in a rich place—rich with opportunity for growth and change. The answer to their prayers may even be hidden in what they are referring to as their misfortune. I am certainly tender with them, but I don't pity someone who is being presented with an opportunity to deepen their faith, understanding and trust in the Universe. The key is that being compassionate with someone out of love carries no strings. Being there for someone out of fear or need—to assure they are in our debt in case we need a favor down the road, or to be able to play the role of hero, carries strings (hidden agendas). This is a love tainted with insecurities (fears) at best. True love cannot be earned, or bought.

"Love cannot be commanded, it cannot be won by force or authority. Only by love is love awakened." ~ Ellen White[2]

Case Study #1

Kim's teacher asked her first grade class to straighten their desks. When Kim's straightening didn't meet her teacher's expectations she dumped everything from Kim's desk onto the floor and then demanded she pick it up. Kim innocently stated that she wasn't going to pick up her things because she hadn't made the mess. Kim's response escalated her teacher's rage to the point of involving the principal, who involved Kim's mother.

Was this a loving way to teach neatness or a selfish opportunity to dump not only the contents of a desk, but some unresolved rage? Was Kim being a selfish brat or respectful toward herself and her teacher? Kim responded from a place pure-of-heart. She honored herself and the teacher by not taking responsibility for her teacher's rage. She hadn't dumped the contents of the desk so she wasn't going to pick them up. It was that simple. The teacher was out of line.

Intimidating Kim by involving her mother and the principal was the teacher's second attempt to dump her rage. Her rage rendered her delusional. Kim was confused about what she had done to necessitate such action and fortunately Kim's mother renewed Kim's faith in herself by supporting her in front of these authorities. This support offered the teacher a more real perspective from which to view the situation.

As adults, as a rule, when feelings are triggered, only about 10-20% is from the current situation and the other 80-90% is old unresolved stuff that the current situation has brought to the surface. Triggers point us in the direction of healing. Clearly, a desk not straightened to a teacher's standards does not warrant shaming the child in front of the entire class by dumping its contents. There must have been some rage already present to have triggered this cascade effect. Using an innocent child as a container for dumping unresolved issues is pretty selfish. Shaming is not loving, but facing our rage can lead to flushing out old wounds, humility, and consequently, purity-of-heart.

Case Study #2

Karen and Carl had been dating for two years. It was common for them to hang out with his friends but being one of the guys was getting old to Karen. When friends called Carl to go out he would, but if Karen wanted to do something he was usually too tired.

Karen's attempts to communicate her frustration were met by Carl's defensiveness. She threw her hands up in the air and started going out with some girls from work. Karen began meeting people with similar interests and felt alive again. She was attracting people who reflected her renewed sense of self-worth and in the process noticed that she was developing feelings for someone new.

This new friend had revealed what she was missing in her relationship with Carl and her findings stirred even more bitterness and confusion toward him. She couldn't help but initially blame Carl for feeling insignificant and unappreciated, while rewarding her new friend for making her feel valuable. But the truth was that the change had taken place inside of Karen and her outer world was just reflecting it. Karen's relationship with Carl reflected her belief that love calls for sacrifice and her relationship with the new guy reflected how great it felt to be herself.

Carl had put Karen's needs aside to meet his own. Given Karen's choice to voluntarily sacrifice her desires to be with him, it was a match made in heaven. Nothing was getting resolved because the deeper issues that were causing the problems weren't being addressed. Over time Karen gave up on expressing her frustration and began to withdraw.

Karen had never ventured beyond her frustration, but as we peeled back the layers, feelings of hurt, insignificance, worthlessness, hopelessness and inadequacy surfaced. There was an accumulation of these unexpressed feelings and the trail went all the way back to her childhood.

Karen's first step toward loving more purely was to forgive herself for her choice to sacrifice and the cascade of unhappy emotions that stemmed from it. If Karen doesn't take responsibility for her part it will only be a matter of time before she creates a Karen-and-Carl dynamic with the new guy.

Karen longed to love and to be loved, but her hidden agenda of sacrificing to earn love and to hold onto Carl was fear-based and selfish.We cannot have compassion for someone when we are taking his or her behavior personally. Karen needed Carl to do things with her to feel valuable, yet he was busy attempting to maintain his relationships with his guy friends who couldn't relate to him having a serious girlfriend. Karen, as one of the guys, seemed to solve the problem for Carl, but not for Karen.

Karen had not considered Carl except in respect to how she wanted him to respond to her and vice versa. They both had hidden agendas that were hidden even from themselves.

As Karen was able to forgive herself for sacrificing, along with all the pain it had created, her relationship with Carl began to shift. She did need some distance from Carl as she processed her feelings because of all the pain she had allowed to accumulate over the course of two years, yet she felt hopeful for both of their futures. The more she loved the wounded parts of herself that feared losing Carl rather than sacrificing to avoid her fear, the more Carl and others were able to respond to her in the loving way her heart desired.

As Karen owned her part, she was able to respond to Carl with compassion rather than frustration. During their separation Carl matured too. He was able to be honest with his friends about his desire to spend quality time with Karen. A truer, purer, more mature love emerged between them. Changing their attitudes about love took their relationship to new heights.

As Karen continues to go deep within herself for her answers, and takes responsibility for her beliefs and attitudes about love, she can respond from a place more pure-of-heart. The more true she is to herself rather than sacrificing, the safer she feels and the more able she is to experience what unfolds without being attached to a particular outcome.

From this more pure-of-heart place, she only wants what is the highest and best for her and for Carl. If that means moving forward together, great, and if it means separating, she trusts that that can be great too. She doesn't need a guaranteed outcome for their future together because she knows that the more she loves herself, the more love she will attract, and she feels safe in that process. There will still be a grieving process because their old relationship is dying, but Karen is learning to trust that in time a new relationship together or apart will take its place as long as her heart so desires.

If Karen didn't want to take responsibility for her sacrificing, she could blame Carl and go forward into a relationship with someone new who initially will make her feel important. Yet she would eventually repeat her experience of feeling hurt and insignificant because these are the feelings that cascade from her sacrificing for love.

Some people spend their lives selfishly looking for Mr. or

Ms. Right, that one who will finally make them feel important. What they don't realize is that the process begins with them.

From Survival Mode to Conscious Mode

We often find ourselves transitioning from survival mode to conscious mode on our journey toward becoming pure-of-heart. In survival mode choices tend toward being fear-based and selfish. When not directly connected to a deeper understanding of how our energy manifests in the world, we can only trust choices based on our past history. We may talk the talk of being connected to something more, but we will be unable to genuinely trust and lean on that relationship. Trusting solely on what we perceive to be *logical* limits our possibilities for solutions, causes us to hold out for guarantees that never come, and often evolves into controlling behavior as a substitute for the safety that comes with genuine loving.

In conscious mode we know and trust in our personal connection with Truth and Love. We are open to solutions our logical mind can't fathom and look forward to their unfolding. In facing our fear, there is no need for a guarantee. We are aware that our past history sometimes shows up in our current circumstances and we know the value in addressing both. We take responsibility for all our creations and the emotions fueling them because we know that the effort it takes to be pure-of-heart is rewarding beyond measure and anything less is futile.

In Conclusion

The selfish-of-heart long to be loved, but are hurtful in their process. Since their intentions are survival-based, their thoughts, words and actions can be destructive. They justify, defend and blame in an effort to convince themselves and others that their intentions are necessary and honorable. By denying the wounded feelings that fuel their actions, they consciously or unconsciously dump those feelings onto others and if they are met with resistance, as with Kim's teacher, they will justify, defend and blame in a last ditch effort to be right.

It is impossible to come from a place that is pure-of-heart when we harbor unprocessed emotions from situations in the past with similar essence. It is hard to discern our pain from the pain of others. Rather than bury emotions we will want to learn to embrace them in order to genuinely be there in a loving way for others—just don't give those emotions decision-making authority as Kim's teacher did when she dumped the contents of Kim's desk. When feelings arise explore them with interest rather than reacting to them. Utilize triggered emotions as a guide to a situation from the past that is ripe for closure. A phrase such as, "Let me get back to you," can buy us the time necessary to purify our hearts and respond with love. If Kim's teacher had backed off and responded to her rage rather than reacting to it, she would have realized why she was taking Kim's lack of *neatness* so personally. She could have come back grateful for her findings and with loving authority toward Kim.

Sometimes we can genuinely be loving and sometimes we can't. When we can't it is time to purify our hearts by taking responsibility for the reasons that are preventing or blocking our ability to love. Truth without love is condescending, and love without truth is enabling. But truth with love is liberating. Healing in its truest sense involves changing some of our deepest and most basic limiting attitudes about love.

Why me? Why now? Why not?

Questions to inspire loving versus selfish behaviors:

- *Have you been disappointed by someone's behavior toward you?*

- *What might they be showing you about your own beliefs and attitudes on love?*

- *Any worthy pursuit takes practice. To venture on the pure-of-heart path, slow down and ask yourself prior to speaking or acting, "Am I coming from a place of fear or love?" If you believe it to be fear, sit with it. If you believe it to be love, act on it. Practice will test your accuracy and a coach or counselor will save trial and error time and maybe even a relationship or two.*

Forgiveness is a gift to the one who forgives.

Chapter 4
Have I Forgiven?
8 Check Points On The Journey

Have you ever thought you had forgiven someone until the subject came up and you realized it still had an emotional charge?

Forgiveness is a journey toward freedom from our past. It can be transformational, complex, is not to be taken lightly and cannot be commanded. It requires effort, discipline and soul-searching. When patient and open to the unfolding of forgiveness, a desire to forgive will be fulfilled.

You will know you have reached your desired destination when only love and gratitude remain in your heart for the person you have forgiven. When a hurtful past relationship has been transformed into an opportunity for personal growth and healing for which you are grateful—with or without an apology—then you know you are free.

There are check points in the process of forgiveness— points where you may be lulled into premature forgiveness— periods where you are called to check in with yourself in order to move forward on the forgiveness path. You may encounter none or you may encounter them all, but each one can free you from a misconceived notion obstructing genuine forgiveness.

1. Sorry

Does an apology really mend hurt feelings?

Andy (seven-years-old) pushed his sister, Deb (eight-years-old). Mom robotically responded, "Tell your sister you're sorry." In the moment that Mom barked her command, Andy wasn't feeling particularly remorseful. In his mind he had acted in self-defense so his obedient "sorry" came through gritted teeth. His lack of sincerity was so obvious that Mom couldn't resist seizing the moment to make a point. She commented with neutrality, "You might as well have said, F-you."

Since Mom was not one to swear, you can imagine the wide-eyed responses from her young children, but that day changed her relationship with forgiveness forever as well as changing the course of her children's lives. Mom sought the aid of a counselor to help resolve the fighting because, clearly, *sorry* alone could not mend hurt feelings, provide peace of mind, or permanently resolve a conflict.

Mom learned the value of listening to both sides, which revealed how Deb could sometimes push Andy with her words. She never rushed her children into an apology or into accepting one again. Instead she began sending them both out for a lap around the house to cool off at the onset of an argument.

An apology is an admittance of guilt. It can assist with reconciliation but it does not help with forgiveness, mend hurt feelings, provide peace of mind, or permanently resolve a conflict. Owning our contribution to the conflict, finding purpose and implementing positive changes does.

2. The Why Versus The How

Hurtful behavior is *how* pain, confusion and ignorance spill over onto others. While some behaviors are just plain unforgivable, the person behind them is not. For forgiveness to work, that is, to free us, it requires an understanding of *why* we have been wronged. If we have taken the situation personally, we must be willing to acknowledge and release ourselves from any other emotional bondage that the event has stirred up for us.

Emotional bondage? Stirred up for us? How does that happen?

Pressured by his superiors, George's boss, Steve, called a department meeting. He reprimanded George for his recent lack of performance in front of the entire group. George just wanted to curl up in a ball. Feelings of inadequacy brought him back to sixth grade when his history teacher had reprimanded him in front of the entire class for failing to

42

hand in his homework assignment, again.

What the teacher hadn't known was that George's parents were in the midst of a messy divorce and that George was caught in the crossfire. This time Steve didn't know that George's wife had recently been diagnosed with stage IV cancer.

Steve felt wronged by his employee. His bosses had come down on him, in part, because of George's poor performance. He was unable to forgive George as long as he is focused on *how* he has been wronged. With his job on the line and unaware of George's wife's condition, it appeared to him as though George had let him down.

Forgiveness requires gathering all our information. Steve was missing the *why*. He came down on George for slacking (the how) without ever asking *why* his performance had recently been lacking.

George was struggling to digest the disturbing news of his wife's illness; hence he hadn't shared. Feeling like a victim he proceeded to put his boss down for embarrassing him. But George didn't know that his boss was being pressured by his superiors.

At age twelve, George didn't have the maturity to understand or explain how his parents' fighting was affecting his homework. Rather than ask, his teacher assumed George was slacking. Who knows what else might have been going on in his teacher's life at the time?

Are you seeing some parallels? Are you seeing how a current situation can stir up our history? Can you see how George could be grateful for Steve's faux pas if he utilizes it as an opportunity to flush out this old wound, to forgive and to mature?

When George revisited his childhood experience he realized that his teacher was not aware of what was distracting George from doing his homework and that he likely had his own troubles. He finally has the missing pieces necessary to understand, forgive and to apply what he has learned to his current circumstances. George could ask Steve why he's so upset as well as inform him of his own circumstances rather than jumping to conclusions. George and his boss could both grow because of this or despite this misunderstanding—if they so choose.

3. The Perpetrator-Victim Conundrum

Believing we are victims keeps us stuck in terms of personal development, spiritual growth and forgiveness. This is a tough checkpoint to move beyond, but to do so is transformational, enlightening and freeing. We have all been perpetrator and victim at one time or another.

Can you see how George had been both in his situation?

He was victim because his boss had come down on him; perpetrator because he had come down on his boss by venting to his colleagues; and both situations occurred without all the facts.

My intention is not to be insensitive to victims. I am just suggesting being open to the possibility that there is more than one perspective. When we focus on healing our own wounds, we begin to see ourselves in our perpetrators, and can forgive them and ourselves for having become the self-centered beings that our harbored pain, confusion and ignorance can turn us into. Forgiveness is our bridge from separation to oneness.

Once George could see himself in his boss, he was one step closer to forgiveness. Realizing that this was his ticket to healing this childhood wound provided the last leg of his journey. He saw purpose. Only love and gratitude were left in his heart: love in the form of compassion for himself and his boss for reacting before they had the entire picture in front of them, and gratitude for the circumstances that sent him back into his past for healing and closure.

Being on the 'victim' end of pain we have inflicted onto others, or on the 'perpetrator' end of pain that has been inflicted onto us, are both powerful places from which to activate forgiveness.

4. Reconciliation Versus Forgiveness

The most important point to grasp is that forgiveness is a gift to the one who forgives. It frees the forgiver from the past through understanding. Forgiveness does not condone hurtful behavior. It is distinct from reconciliation in that it does not require the participation of the perpetrator.

Reconciliation takes two. When a perpetrator can take responsibility for the feelings that fueled her actions and the victim can take responsibility for the feelings that attracted the situation and fueled his response, there is the potential for growth and healing individually and in the relationship.

Vaughn had expressed his desire to make time for Theresa following the completion of the workshop he was facilitating. When Saturday came, Theresa was excitedly anticipating their time together only to find that the promise had slipped Vaughn's mind, once again. Theresa was disappointed, hurt and angry for making time and her effort not being reciprocated as planned. Vaughn used the excuse that he had been exhausted following the workshop and had slept most of the day. But what was really going on?

In Theresa's search for understanding she had an epiphany. "When I say I'll do something, I've thought it through. I'm expecting Vaughn to think like me and disappointed when he doesn't."

She had been projecting this talent onto Vaughn and been repeatedly disappointed rather than seeing him for who he was, a man with good intentions but poor follow-through because he didn't know how to think things through first.

A few weeks later ...

Vaughn finishes sharing several pressing deadlines with Theresa. When she mentions some ideas for her brochure Vaughn suggests some software that Theresa is unfamiliar with and eagerly offers his assistance. This time Theresa sees Vaughn. She acknowledges his good intentions along with his list of deadlines and asks if he genuinely thinks there will be time for both. With Theresa's help, Vaughn was able to reassess the situation, renege his offer and make plans to teach Theresa the software at a later date that worked for both of them.

Reconciliation is usually reserved for more intimate relationships such as family, friends and intimate partners. It involves inviting the perpetrator of pain back into your heart. When genuine, the perpetrator will want to show you how he has healed and developed to become worthy of that honor. But for the reconciliation to be complete you must be willing to share how you also have healed and developed as a result of his painful prompting.

In this case, Theresa learned to accept Vaughn rather than project her *talent* onto him and be disappointed because he's not her. Vaughn learned some tips from Theresa to help him make more deliberate and thoughtful decisions. Such reconciliation requires soul-searching on both ends, but this pursuit empowers individuals while deepening the intimacy between them like nothing else you could ever imagine.

5. Pretense

Authentic forgiveness, as we have just seen, is a soul-searching process that takes genuine effort. However there is also such a thing as inauthentic or false forgiveness, which is a form of arrogance. You may be able to fool someone into thinking you have forgiven them, but it is impossible to forgive someone without going through the process of understanding that there is pain and fear behind the perpetrator's act and that you have somehow unknowingly contributed to the conflict. Pretense feeds egos; forgiveness feeds hearts.

Some people think they are practicing forgiveness by attempting to be the bigger person; others who claim to have forgiven are avoiding conflict and the attention it draws, and some would rather shortcut the forgiveness process than admit to the seemingly insurmountable hurt that it stirred in them from their past history. Pretense boosts pride while humility promotes healing.

"Every person, all the events of your life are there because you have drawn them there. What you choose to do with them is up to you." ~ Richard Bach[3]

Avoiding conflict, playing the role of the "better" person, and hiding from old wounds are substitutes for forgiveness. Real forgiveness entails deep self-awareness: Theresa got it: she saw what needed healing and understanding within herself, and was able to set herself free. The reconciliation was the frosting on the cake. In seeking it, she and Vaughn were both able to set themselves free.

It takes humility to admit that we took something personally; that we have been a perpetrator; that we have felt that way before; and it takes humility to forgive. In order to pass this check point, we must make peace with our pride and muster up the humility necessary to admit that we aren't ready to forgive, or are struggling to do so, and stop pretending that we already have.

6. Feeling Sorry For Someone Versus Forgiveness

Forgiving someone because you feel sorry for him or her is also more an act of arrogance than of forgiveness because it amounts to looking down on them and assuming they aren't capable of changing. Sometimes in our attempt to forgive a family member we may go through the phase of *feeling sorry* for him or her in an attempt to keep them in our lives. This may get us through the holidays, but it won't free us from our past.

Feeling sorry for someone honors neither that person nor our own selves. Feeling sorry can only, at best, feed their self-pity and our arrogance. We must move from arrogance to humility, from pity to compassion, and then surrender the outcome of the relationship if we are to move from this check point.

7. Emotional Charge

If talking about an event or person stirs feelings of anger, pain, shame or makes you cringe at the thought of a repeat performance, there is still an emotional charge. You may have touched the top layers, but there is more to explore. Healing at the root may entail peeling back layers that involve similar pain from past experiences with others, potentially leading back to childhood events.

Lynne was stuck in an unhealthy relationship and quite frustrated with herself by the time she got to my office. Her friends couldn't understand why she kept going back to Nick; their disapproval just added feelings of shame and abandonment to her frustration and confusion.

Probing revealed that Lynne had harbored feelings from the loss of a sibling at the tender age of six. Due to this unresolved experience, feelings of abandonment were so supercharged that she would go to great lengths to avoid being the cause or effect of it, including remaining in relationships that were unhealthy.

Once she was able to connect the dots to her childhood, Lynne was able to use her current circumstances as an opportunity to flush out this old wound along with a few others. She wanted Nick to change so that she wouldn't have to be the perpetrator of *abandonment*. She didn't want to be the cause or the recipient of the pain that she had experienced. Now that the reason she had remained in this unhealthy relationship was crystal clear she was able to replace her frustration with tenderness and self-forgiveness.

From this new vantage point she could see that although Nick appeared confident, his cutting remarks were his insecure feelings spilling over onto her. She understood why she had attracted him, was able to forgive him, accept him for who he was, and end the relationship once and for all for the good of both of them. She was able to move on with love and gratitude in her heart for Nick and all she had learned, how she had healed, and for finally being liberated from the chains of her fear of abandonment. Lynne was seeing with new eyes.

If you are struggling to move beyond the past, don't judge yourself or fall into the trap of judging others. Be honest with yourself and find a professional who can help you to utilize your less-than-optimal circumstances as a springboard to freedom.

8. Self-Forgiveness

In order to forgive another we have to be willing to admit that there have been times when we too have acted inappropriately. We must be willing to explore the pain, confusion and ignorance that provoked our hurtful thoughts, words and/or actions. In the case study above, Lynne was not acting out of love in her relationship with Nick, she was acting out of pain, confusion, ignorance and a fear-of-abandonment, all of which are hurtful.

In order to know that someone else can change we, ourselves, must have experienced the true change that comes from soul-searching rather than the superficial change that comes from merely *controlling* our behavior. Most humbly, in order to forgive a perpetrator we must admit that we, too, have been a perpetrator.

Lynn was able to admit her role as a perpetrator of pain in her relationship with Nick, forgive herself, and finally release them both from the continued perpetrator/victim cycle they had been trapped in.

In Conclusion

Pride clogs the pores of the heart.

Those experiences that are the most challenging to forgive contain the seeds to our greatest liberation. The healing and understanding that accompany forgiveness free our hearts to live more, love more and be more of who we truly are. A devoted journey toward forgiveness can offer us a whole new lease on life. We emerge from these challenges with humility and clarity—seeing purpose where there once was confusion, order where we previously could only see chaos, and similarities where we could only see differences.

Forgiveness does not require an apology, resuming a relationship, or contacting those involved. It does require feeling compassion for the pain, confusion and ignorance that fuels hurtful behaviors. And while the perpetrator is not obliged to face up to his own behavior, neither are you obliged to be further impacted by it. Consequently, forgiveness sometimes requires soul-searching, brutal honesty and connecting current circumstances to past history. It's a process.

When you can ride the emotional charge of pain into your depths and emerge with the joy of healing and growth in your heart, only love and gratitude will remain for yourself and for those you have forgiven.

Why me? Why now? Why not?

Questions to inspire your own forgiveness journey:

- *Who might you be struggling to forgive?*

- *What checkpoint are you stuck on?*

- *How can you be more because of this experience?*

- *What might you have contributed to the situation?*

- *What part of the perpetrator's experience can you understand, empathize with and relate to?*

A spiritual approach to any pursuit—even one as seemingly mundane or material as weight loss—always brings us to a deeper truth.

Chapter 5
Naked Truth: Weight Loss and Our Relationship with God

Since each of us is simultaneously a physical and spiritual being, everything in our lives, every problem we confront, has both a physical and spiritual aspect. Even those things that seem purely physical in nature, such as our bodies, are, in truth, also spiritual. It makes sense then that if we go deeply into our relationship with our physical selves we will soon find ourselves in the realm of spirit. At the root of everything lies our relationship with God. We find this divinity wherever we look, even when we look into our most bodily selves as we struggle with weight problems.

A spiritual approach to any pursuit—even one as seemingly mundane or material as weight loss—always brings us to a deeper truth. Sometimes people who have an aversion to God or religion are drawn to this deeper truth, while others who profess to be religious are secretly avoiding the truth. We can be in denial or unaware of the existence of God or of truth, but that doesn't diminish the existence of either.

The crucial thing to realize is that the realm of Spirit is the realm of Truth. Here we cannot pretend to be something we are not; we cannot be in denial of our choices and the fruits they bear. Being brutally honest with ourselves is standing naked before God. As long as we hide behind our proverbial clothes or avoid the scale of Truth, we cannot have a close relationship with our Creator.

Applying The Principles Of Denying Truth To Weight Gain

If seeking truth brings us closer to God, then avoiding truth separates us. That separation from God can manifest itself as weight gain. When we go through a period of eating poorly we typically avoid the truth-teller scale. That is, we avoid standing naked—admitting to our deeper feelings and facing the fruit of our choices.

The guilt many people feel around weight gain is often really anger toward themselves—which can only serve to send them plummeting deeper into bad feelings. The guilt-burdened person typically either continues to avoid the scale (to avoid facing the truth) or uses the rising numbers as a form of self-punishment—both tactics simply reinforce their feeling of failure. Subsequently, people will often gain even more weight; hence the downward spiral. Feeling bad created the weight in the first place, and feeling worse just adds more weight. The person literally becomes weighed down with guilt. When merely fighting the scale to control the numbers, we are likely to eventually find ourselves lost in shame, denial and further from the truth.

I initially attempted to come to grips with weight through control. I remember telling myself that I would eat better and weigh myself in a few days, but I failed to address why I was eating poorly in the first place: I didn't stand naked before myself and God—I just controlled my choices better. There was no learning, no healing and no growth. While common sense tells us that weight loss requires greater self-control, the spiritual truth is that if we are only in a contest with ourselves for control, we are not really standing naked before God. As long as we are focused on controlling ourselves, we are not ready to surrender ourselves to our divinity.

We are ready to face the scale when we are ready to own our choices and the results of those choices, forgive ourselves, have compassion, and make changes in how we live and cope. If we just control the weight with exercise and diet, we are likely to find ourselves here again or in some other struggle at some point in the future because we haven't learned what our weight gain was truly about.

Applying The Principles Of Seeking Truth To Weight Loss

When weight is the issue brought in by a client, we use it as an opportunity to learn, heal and grow. Once the intention has been set to address the message brought forth by excess weight, the client is taught to identify and embrace the universe's responses to her request. Our prayers are always answered, but there is no shortcut to permanent transformation. True transformation is a journey requiring effort, discipline and surrender. It is fulfilling and rewarding on every level from physical to spiritual. We may have to distance ourselves from those who share the habits we no longer desire for a period of time, but when our healthier eating becomes nonnegotiable, it will either be respected, motivate those around us, or lead us to healthier, more inspiring relationships.

The universe's response to a request for weight loss will likely present opportunities to confront living habits on the mental, emotional and spiritual levels. This will take us to unfinished business from our past that is impeding our adult journey. This is where we stand naked before ourselves and God—where we speak our most urgent truth to begin the journey that will lead deep within ourselves.

Physical truth: Sheila's most urgent truth was that she was making poor eating choices.

Emotional truth: Acknowledging this led her to her next truth: that she eats for comfort when she is stressed. Then it was necessary for her to face the things that trigger her stress, and allow herself to experience the stressful emotions she was escaping and learn to process them.

Mental truth: This brought her to childhood memories of verbal abuse that had stripped her of her self-esteem. She had concluded that she was stupid and worthless and this belief had greatly impeded her journey.

Spiritual truth: Once we lifted the veil of shame and pain this belief had created, she saw the low self-esteem of her perpetrators and that she had been their scapegoat. The wound was exposed. She had been blamed for the worthlessness of others and had carried their pain as her own. She also saw that she was abusing herself with food. She had unknowingly designated her body as her scapegoat.

Standing naked before herself and God, Sheila requested love, forgiveness and healing. She saw the truth and was able to forgive her perpetrators for allowing their pain to spill over onto her. She was also able to forgive herself for the fruit of her own pain. This changed and liberated her.

With every step Sheila took toward truth, God shed more light. She emerged more loved and empowered with wisdom, understanding and compassion that she could thrive on.

Avoiding the pain of worthlessness had come to consume

Sheila and the truth had set her free. This is fulfillment at its best. When we let go of false beliefs about ourselves, space is opened in our hearts and minds for God to fill with Love and Truth. We no longer need extra sweets to make up for a lack of affection, fatty foods to cushion potential blows from abuse, or carbs to stifle our passion. We see our feelings as fuel for growth and healing and learn how to use them to experience God at work in our lives.

Walking this path allows us to witness how our relationship with our world is divinely orchestrated based on our intentions rather than being random and chaotic as we once thought. From here we can adopt new eating habits that nurture our new state of being.

Once the real issues are addressed, eating healthily is easy and enjoyable because there is no longer a purpose to unhealthy eating choices. Furthermore, when we find ourselves in an unhealthy eating pattern or some other struggle in the future, we know that it is just a heads-up from the universe, a signal that it is time to confront a truth that will bring us into even deeper intimacy with ourselves and God.

Applying The Principles Of Seeking Truth To God

Going deep brings us closer to God because it allows us an opportunity to stand naked before Him—open, honest and free of our proverbial clothes (the coverings that come between us and the truth: the various ways we avoid exposing our real selves). This is head-to-toe intimacy with God: naked on the physical, emotional, mental and spiritual levels.

Removing our proverbial clothes is the first step toward total spiritual nakedness. In meditation we can invite God to bear witness. Here we can reveal the details of what happened (physical), how it felt (emotional), the story we told ourselves about the incident based on our past experience (mental), why we attracted the situation and exposure of that old wound for healing and growth (spiritual). Standing naked before God is inviting God to touch us, with wisdom, understanding, healing, joy and ultimately with Love in all its many forms. It invites God to shed light where there was darkness, to offer healing where there were wounds, and to bring understanding where there was confusion.

In Conclusion

When we make choices based on fear or shame, we are likely to avoid God, the source of Truth and Light, just as we avoid the scale. We don't want this omnipresent force to see us; we flee from the truth as we avoid facing up to our own behavior, whether it's late night snacking or secret stashes of junk food. We tell ourselves we'll talk to God when we are in a better place, just as we postpone pursuing our desires (taking that vacation, buying that dress, going on that interview, seeking that relationship) until we lose a little weight. But avoiding the truth just prolongs our agony by immobilizing us.

When one is on a path to control and avoid feelings, one is also on a path to avoid growth. Losing weight to avoid deeper issues will provide temporary success at best. A problematic issue is a call to go deep. When we heed our call and follow it to that place of naked truth, we will meet God there. Whether we acknowledge this presence or not is our choice, but the view is insightful and humbling regardless.

Regularly standing naked before God is a form of reverence. There really is no point to life if we have no relationship with this Universal Intelligence because it is everywhere. Be it religious, metaphysical or scientific—there is no fighting it, no controlling it, no deceiving it. We can evade it, but only to our own detriment. The truth can be tough to take, and facing it takes courage, effort and discipline—but the exquisiteness of the fruit will keep us coming back for more. In the end, weight loss is not about self-denial but about a deep form of self-affirmation and self-expansion based on a loving relationship with God.

Why me? Why now? Why not?

Questions to inspire an honest relationship with the Divine:

- *Look at yourself in the mirror as if you are looking*

at your own best friend.

- *Do you see someone who has been struggling?*

- *Do you see someone who has been using food to comfort hurt feelings, to pacify boredom or to fill some other void?*

- *Can you have compassion?*

- *What do you want to say to him or her?*

- *Can you get some help with these deeper issues?*

The further we stray from our centers the easier it is to blame our symptoms for our discord rather than thank them for being our personal GPS device calling for us to "recalculate."

Chapter 6
The Health Angel Who Stood By Me

When there is discord of any kind in my life, cleansing the fear from my motives is what provides relief.

When one of my clients was struggling with some health issues it sent me back to revisit some of my own past health issues. I love hindsight because it always provides a 20/20 perspective. I can see both sides of a situation in a way that I couldn't when I was in it.

In the midst of my reflecting I had this image of a health issue personified. It was an overly excited boy knocking at my door. I pictured him running for miles to get a message to me. By the time he finds me he is animated, out of breath and speaking gibberish.

He freaks me out, not only because he's a stranger, but because I thought everything was fine before this babbling messenger showed up to tell me otherwise. In the early days I thought this crazy kid was a troublemaker so I'd call in special forces covered under my HMO to get him off my property (medicate, radiate or surgically remove him).

I had traveled so far off course from being true to myself—from my soul's plan—that I couldn't recognize him for the angel that he was. He had to travel so far and his message was so urgent, that by the time he located me I could only view him as a blubbering idiot. I found this 'disturbed' youth to be an irritation to my blissfulness. But in hindsight I was the disturbed one, my bliss was really my ignorance and he was my Godsend.

When I couldn't get him off my property with my HMO-approved methods, I started opening the door a crack in an attempt to calm him down (physical therapy, chiropractic care, acupuncture, energy work). Once calm he'd want to chat about my living and loving. But I was too anxious to get back on the track that had gotten me sick, so I'd pop a pacifier in his mouth, shut the door and go on my merry, ignorant way.

Traveling further still from my God-given self, my center, my authenticity, I'd eventually encounter another messenger—or maybe it was the same one, morphed into a new form in his creative efforts to gain my attention.

Why?

Because I didn't understand that I was being called to change some self-destructive tendencies which were causing me to stray from my center, from my life's purpose. I hadn't cleansed the fear from my motives because I wasn't aware that my motives were fearful.

Like what?

Like sacrificing my needs and desires in order to remain connected to *loved* ones. If they weren't asking, I was volunteering. I was operating out of fear-of-loss rather than love. That was my autopilot so I wasn't even conscious of it at the time, but that didn't mean that it was harmless, as this health messenger was indicating.

When sacrificing our own needs and desires as a means for maintaining connection leaves us feeling unappreciated, undervalued and/or depleted we are practicing a means of manipulation rather than love. We know we are practicing love when our actions leave us feeling fulfilled, energized and/or at peace, with or without a thank you.

My condition improved with alternative health care but over time I became a slave to the 'maintenance' care and even became skeptical of its value. That was my cue to voluntarily open the door, remove the pacifier and start listening.

The Journey Back

Can we live with abandon if our modus operandi is to merely pacify, outsmart or destroy our messengers?

Can we truly live well if our motivator is fear-of-loss or fear-of-death?

68

My paths to wellness, both traditional and alternative, were legs on the journey back to my center. Facing my fear of losing connection was the final stretch. Thank goodness my health angel didn't give up on me.

I had to learn to make choices that came from a place of love for my life regardless of the risk of losing connection. The process was not unlike that of a bird hatching. No one can do it for us; we have to be ready to step into the light of truth. I had to admit to my fear. Once I returned to my true center, the connections that remained were the authentic ones.

How do I change course?

Begin by slowing down and asking yourself 3 questions:

1. *What am I about to say or do?*
2. *Why am I about to say or do it?*
3. *Am I acting from a place of fear or love?*

When it is fear, explore what you are afraid of and why. Unresolved issues from the past may surface for revisiting. A trained therapist or counselor can help with revealing default autopilots, with healing and with closure of the past.

When we've got love down, we know it and feel it with our whole heart and soul. We can even apply what we've learned to other areas of our lives that are ready for re-authenticating.

The farther we stray from our centers the easier it is to blame our symptoms for our discord rather than thank them for being our personal GPS device—a messenger who tracks us down to guide us home to the land of milk and honey— that place where it feels great to be us because our world reflects our prosperity.

Being our authentic self is easier said than done at times but once we learn how to take a washcloth to our fears, it is the easiest course of all; the healthiest, most noble and most abundant.

If you have utilized a health issue as a springboard into more authentic living you will know exactly what I am talking about. If you haven't yet taken the leap, it might be time to give it a try and allow your messenger to lift you out of your own downward health spiral.

The Health Angel Who Stood By Me

My health angel first got my attention with TMJ (Temporomandibular Joint Dysfunction) at the age of twenty-three. I addressed the condition with physical therapy per the suggestion of my dentist. I even recognized that it had emotional components, but at the time I thought I just needed to be better at controlling my feelings.

Next was high blood pressure. I acknowledged its association with a strained relationship so we moved to create a little distance. With the assistance of my HMO and a little blame and control my high blood pressure resolved itself as had my TMJ. But my methods left my health angel chomping at the bit because neither blame nor control could foster the healing I was seeking—healing on the mental, emotional and spiritual levels.

At age 28 my husband developed cancer. Two years after the completion of his treatments, the emotional trauma caught up with me. I was lacking a means to maneuver through my feelings. I just couldn't shake them and was worn down from trying so I sought assistance. In hindsight I can see my health angel's creativity. He was showing me my inefficiencies in living and loving from an angle that was harder to ignore.

I got over the hump of the trauma with the aid of a traditional counselor. But the piece she couldn't seem to help me with was what to do with my feelings. I knew how I was supposed to respond to situations and I was good at role-playing, but "What about all these feelings?" I asked my counselor. She didn't have an answer, which sent me in pursuit of one.

In the midst of some parenting challenges I developed a sinus condition that turned chronic. We ripped up carpets, refinished hardwood floors and purchased air purifiers. Then one day while waiting in line for my sinus medication at the pharmacy, I picked up a book. I wish I could remember the name, but I lent it to someone I worked with years ago and never got it back. What I do remember is that it broadened my perspective on my sinus condition. The author said that we store anger and unshed tears in our sinuses. I remember thinking to myself, "I'm not an angry person." But I started paying attention.

I rarely let my anger show, but I did get angry inside, and sometimes I'd get angry when someone would hurt me. I should have been crying, but found it interesting that I'd only get as far as anger. This was progress.

TMJ comes from clenching teeth, high blood pressure can be likened to blood boiling, holding in feelings to be strong for others can be likened to a pressure cooker and sinuses are where we store anger and unshed tears. There were some angry adults in my environment growing up. I had vowed to be nothing like them—to never hurt someone with my anger. But since I believed that anger hurts, I proceeded to hurt myself. I was imploding.

So what causes our inauthenticity?

Fear-of-loss.

At the age of thirty-four, a debilitating repetitive strain injury grabbed me by the ankles and wrestled me to the floor. My feelings came up in full force and my intuition sent me on an alternative healing path which included journaling, learning to meditate, yoga, chiropractic care, acupuncture and lots of self-help books. This journey eventually led me out of my Type A personality and into learning to heal and grow through my feelings. Learning to process my feelings helped heal my injury, my sinus condition, some challenging core relationships, and even some financial challenges. Before this injury I didn't have time to feel my feelings, but with the help of my health angel I came to realize that I really didn't have time not to feel them.

In Conclusion

"It is more important to know what sort of person has a disease than to know what sort of disease a person has." ~ Hippocrates[4]

When we numb our pain, we also numb our joy, so feeling my feelings was like a new lease on life. It even led to a career change from business management to holistic counselor because I figured I couldn't be the only one who had been misguided. I wanted everyone to know what they were missing by not feeling their feelings. I wanted them to know that there was a way to feel them productively rather than destructively.

Initially I was in pursuit of healing my health issues, but in hindsight I can see that it was the way I was living and loving that was most in need of healing. Once I received the message and made the changes, my health messengers went away. I wasn't always graceful and sometimes I was downright defiant. I went through bouts of despair and proceeded with baby-steps. It can be and was an arduous process but it was so worth it.

I have come to believe that God will never grant me a miracle at the expense of my personal growth. But when I choose to learn, heal and grow from my experiences, I am choosing to receive God, and allowing miracles to happen. With every issue I address—whether it is physical, social or financial—I emerge with more wisdom, understanding and compassion than I had before. We can't thrive on problems, but we can thrive on the wisdom, understanding and compassion we gain from them.

Why me? Why now? Why not?

Questions to inspire your own healing journey:

- *What health issues are you struggling with?*

- *What message might they be trying to bring you?*

- *How is your mental, emotional and spiritual health?*

- *Are you running from your messengers, or are you listening to their calls for action?*

- *What steps could you take to recalculate toward a healthier way of living and loving?*

The day we ran out of coffee was the day I realized coffee had power over me.

Chapter 7
Coffee, Crystals and Empowerment

Coffee, crystals and empowerment: what's the connection?

When a friend expressed concern over the possibility of becoming dependent on crystals—that they might come to have power over her, my immediate response was, "Anyone or anything we consistently give our power to will eventually have power over us." When crystals are used consistently in lieu of someone's personal growth, that person will come to depend on them, and they could well end up having power over that person. But if we work with them to facilitate our personal growth, they can help us to come into our own power.

Interestingly enough, my relationship with coffee was the example that came to mind in my effort to explain the dynamics of power. During the course of our conversation I realized that many of the principles I learned through my relationships with coffee and crystals are applicable to anyone seeking to reclaim or redeem their power from any dependency or codependency. I hope you can draw from my story as inspiration toward utilizing your own dependency or codependency as the fuel toward empowerment that it can be.

Coffee And Me

As a young adult I drank a lot of coffee. It came to be my antidote for lack of sleep, the social excuse to get together with other mothers, and a beverage with which to warm my starving heart when I was making choices that didn't nurture me.

The day that we ran out of coffee was the day I realized that coffee had come to have power over me. By noon, I had a splitting headache and it was due to —you guessed it— caffeine withdrawal. Coffee had established control over me and I was angry about it. Since I regarded anything having control over me as a fate worse than death, I blamed coffee for my dependency and made the decision to give it up. Fortunately coffee did not take the breakup personally— which made it easier for me to focus on my contribution to the dependency.

I had developed a love-hate relationship with coffee. I loved what it did for me, and the benefits were real. The problem was that the more heavily I relied on coffee, the more power I gave it. As long as drinking coffee was my idea, I loved it, but I hated the idea of having to drink coffee to avoid a headache.

During my trial separation from coffee I reevaluated my existence. Without coffee it was clear that I had been spreading myself much too thin; I was tired and it didn't feel very good to be me. Why had I been trying to be super-everything—super-mom, super-wife, super-friend, basically super-everything except super-caretaker for myself?

In exploring my motivation for trying to be super-everything, some hidden value issues came to light. I had been constantly trying to prove my value to others and it was running me into the ground. I had unknowingly been abusing myself and had become dependent on coffee to keep up the unhealthy pace. Once coffee was out of the picture I could see the cycle for what it was and only then could I see how I was neglecting my own care.

As I embraced the need to take care of myself, regularly scheduling a sitter for my three children became a priority. My kids were great but being a full-time caregiver is draining and I wasn't particularly fond of who I turned into when depleted. During those two hours I would do whatever my heart desired: not errands and not even getting together with friends, but something purely *selfish*—something healthy and rejuvenating for me. Sometimes I would just sit by a lake and read for a couple of hours. I came to realize that I was a better mother, friend, and wife when I took care of myself. Not only was I benefiting from those two hours every other week, but so was everyone I touched because I was becoming more thoughtful and more loving.

Taking this time for myself helped me to see my life with greater clarity; my motivations changed and subsequently so did my choices regarding how I desired to live.

I had learned to:

- better care for myself.

- have better boundaries.

- say "no" out of love.

- and most significantly, I had learned the importance of taking time to tend to my heart.

Tending to my heart led to pursuing and developing new interests, which in turn led to new friendships. Not only was I much more cognizant of the choices I was making, but tending to my heart taught me to be equally mindful of the motivations for my choices.

Our power lies in our capacity to love and be loved. And our capacity to love and be loved is directly related to our capacity to love ourselves. When we care for, value and honor ourselves, we are engaging in an act of love as great as when we care for, value and honor another person.

One of my discoveries as I withdrew from my dependent relationship was that any such relationship diminishes both parties. Not only had I not been honoring myself, but I also had not been honoring coffee. I had not accepted coffee for what it was. I had been using and abusing it as well as myself in my unconscious attempts to feel valuable and connected. These realizations were truly humbling. I redeemed my power by taking back responsibility for my own care and value. My care should never have been coffee's job, and my value should never have needed proving. What revelations!

I have emerged from my healing journey without the need for coffee and without the need to be everything to everyone that coffee was fueling. I have also emerged with a greater understanding of the positive impact that my capacity to love myself provides. When my desire to care for myself, or any desire for that matter, also considers everyone's best interests, we all benefit; and no one and no thing gets used or abused in the process. That is true power in action. In valuing myself I became a more *sincere* everything rather than a *super* everything and it feels so much better.

Eventually coffee and I reconciled. I had grown so much while we were apart. Fortunately coffee didn't hold a grudge and we have created a new relationship based on honor, respect and pure desire. It is so liberating to no longer be dependent. When I find us squeezing in extra visits, I don't beat myself up; I just mindfully let it warm me while I reevaluate my existence. I enjoy a cup of half-decaf / half-regular most mornings. It is no longer a substitute for sleep, an excuse to get together with friends, or the only way to warm my heart. I don't drink it on the run or take it to go. I create time for us because I enjoy it. Coffee has become part of the ritual with which I begin my day. That may change as I change, but for now, it works for me.

In Conclusion

Anything consistently used as a substitute for personal growth will eventually gain power over the person using it, even when that person believes himself or herself to be in control. In order to take my power back from coffee, I had to say "no" to my existing relationship with it. Our trial separation created the space necessary for me to come to terms with the larger issue of my *super*-tendencies. As I said "no" to these tendencies, I took my power back and used it to value myself by taking better care of myself. In taking better care of myself, my attitude toward coffee changed. I no longer need it; I simply enjoy a cup in the morning.

While dependency itself damages our spirit, relationships that ultimately become dependent are often rooted in something authentic and valuable. After all, they are showing us something we desire. Coffee is warm, comforting, a means for engaging with other people, and a stimulant. It was showing me my desire to feel loved, connected and energized. These qualities offered by coffee are all valuable and beneficial, but when we become dependent on the qualities in anything external to ourselves as a substitute for nurturing ourselves, the relationship can become destructive.

Freeing ourselves from dependency doesn't necessarily mean eliminating the person or thing we are dependent on from our lives forever. In my case it wasn't even so much about coffee as it was about using coffee to fuel my super-human tendencies. Once the super-human tendencies were faced and my desires from the relationship were extracted, I was able to reunite with coffee in a healthy way, meaning that our relationship had to be re-established with new parameters and more mindfulness.

While sometimes we can redeem a relationship once we have overcome the dependent aspect of it, some relationships are best left behind. Once the dependency is eliminated and new, more heart-honoring life-choices are made, the decision to move on becomes natural. The person or thing will either fit in with our desire to honor our heart, or fall out of our life. If it falls out, it just means that the purpose of the relationship was complete and that both parties weren't ready to go someplace new together.

In hindsight I can see what I have learned from my relationship with coffee and how I have applied that learning to other relationships, including my relationship with crystals. Crystals show me what I need and help me to develop those qualities within myself. They are not a substitute for my personal growth. Rather than needing them, I have an affinity for them. The mark of a healthy, non-dependent relationship is that it accommodates and nurtures the desire to grow. My journey with coffee has shown me the value of learning, healing and growing through all my relationships—human and otherwise. Unlike the caffeine boost I used to crave, the boost of energy I receive through the process of reclaiming my power is energy from which my spirit can thrive.

Why me? Why now? Why not?

Questions for determining dependency:

- *What might you be giving your power to that is a substitute for growth?*

- *How are you benefiting from it?*

- *What feelings does the thought of a trial separation bring up for you?*

Attempting to fill the emptiness inside ourselves with purchases is fruitless because it creates emptiness in our bank accounts.

Chapter 8
Evaluating Our Economic Spirit: Navigating Through An Economic Downswing

Should I switch back to the chicken with hormones because my husband got laid off?

Some health concerns in our family had prompted me to gravitate toward organic meats and produce and my family had been thriving on them. But, standing at the meat counter on that fall day in 2001, I was facing a new challenge—my husband had recently been laid off and hormone-free, grain-fed, free-range chicken was significantly more expensive than its less responsibly raised counterpart.

In the past ten years it is likely that you have been faced with a similar decision—a decision between what your spirit knew was best and a more affordable alternative. The worst thing that could happen to our economy—and to ourselves— is to allow economics to rule our spirits.

When times are tough or scary, our tendency is to go into self-deprivation mode.

Some things you might initially tell yourself must be cut in the midst of a money crunch include:

- creative pursuits such as crafts, photography or music.

- wellness practices like yoga, organic eating or personal development classes.

- out-of-pocket health and wellbeing services: i.e. massage, acupuncture or counseling.

It is natural to go into fear mode under stressful circumstances, but what if our subsequent choices only serve to make matters worse?

What if we tell ourselves, and others, that we have no other choice than to deny our spirits healthy foods, environmentally friendly products, and the simple pleasures that keep us sane?

Is it necessary to lower our standards, sacrifice our health and wellbeing and support unethical practices for survival's sake?

While these may seem like *logical*, temporary solutions, depriving our spirits won't improve our personal economy or the economy-at-large.

What Can We Do?

We can use economic-downswing-time to:

- re-evaluate our choices.

- live more mindfully, more respectfully and more deliberately.

- distinguish between those things that boost our egos and those that boost our health.

- differentiate between expenditures that merely act as a substitute for spiritual enrichment and those that genuinely nurture the spirit.

Are your choices modeling our existing economy? Or, to paraphrase Mahatma Gandhi, *Are your choices modeling the integrity you wish to see in the economy-at-large?*

Feeding our spirit is satisfying while feeding our ego leaves us greedy for more. What is a genuine source of enrichment to one person may be used as a status symbol for another.

How can we tell the difference?

What feeds spirit is enriching—what feeds ego is indebting.

What if I don't know which is which?

The good news is, even when we don't actually know what is best; we can find comfort in knowing that our desire to be clear on what is best will guide us in the right direction.

How does this work?

We quite literally create our lives with our thoughts and feelings. When our choices are in fear of the worst, it is because that is all our minds can envision. When our choices are in expectation of the best possible outcome, we open to the Macrocosmic Spirit's vision—a vision inaccessible from a fear stance.

Buying responsibly raised chicken was a spirit-rich choice for me. It respected the chicken, my family and modeled the integrity I wished to see practiced in the world. When I opened to the Macrocosmic Spirit's Vision, I asked for it to somehow be within my means.

Purchasing responsibly raised chicken can be used as a status symbol (to feed ego) if we are doing it to draw attention to ourselves—to prove that we are responsibly-minded, have faith in a higher power or are an animal lover. Purchasing responsibly raised chicken because it makes us feel good about ourselves at the end of the day is a source of enrichment—it honors what is important to us and that leaves us feeling fulfilled.

I'm not suggesting that you purchase hormone-free, grain-fed, free-range chicken during your downswing or ever. But I am interested in *your Chicken Story*.

- *What feeds your spirit—what choice makes you feel*

good about yourself while having a positive impact on others, and is a change you'd like to see more of in the world?

- *What happens to your integrity-rich choice in a downswing?*

- *Have you been unknowingly sacrificing your integrity in support of upholding a status symbol?*

Ego Indulgence Versus Spirit Indulgence

Genuine integrity is a reflection of our wholeness and faith, neither of which are economy-sensitive.

Status symbols are our attempts to cover up the debt (the emptiness and insecurity) inside ourselves. Filling our emptiness with attention in this way only transfers the debt to our credit cards. Even when a status symbol appears to be paid for, something else will suffer because of it. Investing in status symbols indulges the ego. It supports the thriving of a robbing-from-Peter-to-pay-Paul mentality—it blocks economic flow and turns our back toward Spirit-rich possibilities.

Sometimes we can only figure out which are our status symbols and which are our sources of enrichment in hindsight. But if we didn't risk putting ourselves out there, how would we know? If we couldn't shed light on our emptiness how would we know we weren't whole?

Economic downswings provide time for indulging our spirits:

- Rid your living space of items that are no longer a source of enrichment.

- Utilize a status symbol as a marker for retrieving lost self-esteem.

- Pursue a desire to model integrity and follow it through to the end.

- Face your fears rather than giving them the car keys.

- Desire best across the board and call on Macrocosmic Spirit's Vision for guidance.

National Economy Versus Household Economy

According to Merriam Webster the word "economy" is defined as "the management of household or private affairs and especially expenses."

The economy— of a household or a society—is the result of our choices. Reacting to a financial downfall with more of what brought it down won't bring it back. However, if we *learn* from our financial mistakes and the mistakes of others, they can serve as a springboard into greater joy—bringing about growth and evolution.

One place to start is to notice any stories from the

macrocosmic economy that fill you with warmth, admiration or hope. That positive response signals the reflection of a quality you want to bring forth in yourself or an ethic you would like to adopt. For example, the news story of a child raising money for a cause he or she believes in and all the support that springs forth, could inspire you to pursue a passion.

On the other hand, pay close attention to what bothers you most about the current economic crisis—what really gets under your skin. These are often the exact things we don't like about ourselves that are ready for changing. For example, a manufacturer gets called out for selling a defective product. Their attempt to cut costs at the expense of humanity's wellbeing could inspire you to explore the effects of your attempts to cut costs on your family's health and/or wellbeing. Understood in this way, the national economy can help us to heal our household economies.

How Can I Make Spirit-Rich Financial Choices?

To facilitate the shift from win-lose (displacing debt) to win-win (creating mutual wealth), slow down and act mindfully and deliberately rather than automatically and reactively. Regularly pause, reflect and ask some serious questions prior to spending such as:

- *Is this money I am about to spend constructive or*

destructive to myself, those around me and the environment?

- *Am I motivated out of love or out of fear?*

- *Do my possessions and purchases serve to uplift me (feed my spirit) or merely to impress my neighbors (feed my ego)?*

When the motivation behind any act is spirit-based, we have consideration for the highest and best for all involved, including ourselves; we intend for harm to no one.

The Challenge

In times of transition it can be hard to know what is of the highest and best intent.

When confused, simply direct your will toward the good. Admit if you can't picture being able to afford what you desire. Then be open for it or its equivalent (or better) to come in an affordable way.

It takes practice and discernment to learn to trust this mindset, but know that a sincere desire for good is always a positive contribution to humanity. When the motivation behind an act is fear-based it means we only have our own best interests at heart. Fear often leads us to try to exercise control—over others, over ourselves, over our environment.

Case Study:

Jonathan's unemployment was running out so he downplayed his concern over the condescending attitude of a potential employer and accepted the job, only to experience spiritual bankruptcy down the road as he was robbed of his sense of self-worth.

When acting from fear, look to what you are trying to protect yourself from—what you are trying to prevent from manifesting. It is likely a repeat performance of something you have already experienced. The irony is that by attempting to avoid the thing we fear, we are in fact feeding that fear, which makes it more likely to actualize. In the above example, Jonathan's fear of bankruptcy actualized, just in a different way than he had pictured. Buying into our fears steers us away from the guidance of Spirit.

Acknowledging our fear or doubt is the first step down the win-win path. I'm not suggesting that Jonathan should or shouldn't have taken the job, just that he could have avoided spiritual bankruptcy.

How?

If he owns his part (admitting to himself, hence to Spirit, that there was too much fear to wait for something else to come along) and asks Spirit for the highest outcome his focus can shift from cutting his losses to accepting what there is to gain from the experience.

When fear rules us win-lose solutions are all we can access.

When faith rules us win-win solutions become available.

With a little integrity (being honest about his fear) Jonathan's job could have been utilized as a bridge from fear to faith.

Discerning Spiritual Value

Trying to discern the spiritual value of a given expenditure requires, above all, that we be honest with ourselves. For example, a car or home purchased to prove our success to others is a non-spiritual choice because it is based on a fear that others see us as inferior. Any choice such as this that is designed to prove something to others is ego-based. When a car is reliable, pleasing to the eye and to the pocketbook—purchased in win-win fashion—it uplifts the spirit. It is a choice based in love.

The same goes for a house. It can be a home, a place of nurturance, creativity and peace, or it can be a McMansion way beyond the means of the buyer—and we have seen where that has gotten us.

Behavior that feeds the ego reveals debt because it is based in debt (the feeling of lack). *Purchases to prove* are attempts to hide the debt—the perceived absence of personal value—inside ourselves.

Feeding ego is not unlike attempting to feed an insatiable monster; it is like throwing money into a black hole. We overspend ourselves into debt because we are trying to fill an emptiness that can't be filled from the outside. Robbing from Peter to pay Paul is a *zero-sum* mindset. Attempting to fill the emptiness inside ourselves with purchases is fruitless because it creates emptiness in our bank accounts.

On the other hand, filling the emptiness by retrieving something inside of ourselves that has been lost or abandoned is a *non-zero-sum* solution. We use the debt as a messenger to retrieve some of our lost value—some of the uniqueness we gave up in our efforts to belong—and emerge with more of ourselves.

Investments In Spirit

Thinking of our purchases as investments (much as we think of stocks and mutual funds) can help us get perspective by elongating our timeline. Instead of choosing instant gratification, we *choose to choose* that which yields long-term dividends. This will lead us towards more ethical choices in our own lives, which will be reflected in the larger economy.

When we are only looking for the *best deal* in the short-term we come from a place of greed or fear of lack. On the other hand, when we look simply for *the best* and for it to be within our means, we are coming from a place of riches.

An example of an investment in spirit would be money or time spent in support of something that brings us joy. That could be:

- time surrounded by art or practicing an art.

- time in nature that stabilizes our spirit—mountains, rivers, a lake, the beach.

- listening to uplifting music or viewing artistic performances.

- time and/or money spent (within our means) on food or activities that will improve our health.

These kinds of expenditures are investments in long-term well-being—in choices that support wholeness. They positively impact us (they inspire, uplift and balance us) and everyone we touch by proxy. Moreover, feeling good about ourselves magnetizes good things to us, so this type of investment reaps far-reaching benefits.

The feeling associated with a short-term purchase in an attempt to fill a sense of emptiness such as *retail therapy*, is akin to an adrenaline rush. It may be nice while it lasts but it quickly diminishes, leaving us feeling emptier than before.

A long-term investment that feeds the spirit such as acquiring a piece of art that uplifts and inspires, registering for a series of meditation classes or selling or donating items that are ready to move on—is a gift that keeps on giving.

Sometimes we gather our information, make our best decision and put both feet in, only to realize that our choice was a choice toward more debt rather than more wholeness—a choice that took away from others in our effort to fill ourselves rather than a choice that made us and everyone involved more whole, more empowered, more wealthy in spirit. In these cases, we can pick ourselves up, dust ourselves off, forgive ourselves and then fine-tune, tweak or completely change course.

In Conclusion

There are plenty of things that we do not have the power to change during an economic downswing. Focusing on these things can only feed feelings of powerlessness, hopelessness, helplessness and despair.

"Trust in the Lord with all your heart and lean not on your own understanding; in all your ways acknowledge Him, and He will direct your paths." (Proverbs 3:5-6 NKJV)[5]

Ask for a win-win and surrender the outcome to the Macrocosmic Spirit. In the meantime focus on what you do have the power to change. Downswings provide us with time to reevaluate our economic spirits—to let go of what no longer serves us physically, mentally, emotionally and spiritually. Be sure to replace it with what will serve your personal economy and the economy-at-large by proxy.

Honor and nurture your spirit and the reflections will be awe-inspiring. Lie to your spirit and your world will reflect your deception. The principle at work is not one of reward and punishment: it is the principle of karma—we reap what we sow—our thoughts, words and actions are reflected in our personal worlds and globally by proxy.

Denial gets us nowhere. Truth—facing the truth, admitting the truth, acting on the truth—will finally set us free. These are complex times; the issues we face can threaten to overwhelm us. The solution is to take one step at a time out of win-lose displaced debt and into win-win creation of healthy wealth. We may not always know what is best, but when our desire is to meet our needs in a way that enriches our spirits while simultaneously enriching the spirits of others, ideas on how to proceed will come flooding in. One thing we can be sure of is that Spirit will always come back with win-win solutions. If it's not win-win, then the solution is coming from someplace else.

Why me? Why now? Why not?

Questions to inspire a win-win attitude:

- *When making an expenditure am I acting in full consciousness?*

- *Are my financial choices modeling the integrity I wish to see in the economy-at-large?*

- *What do my spending behaviors and/or the behaviors of others indicate about how I am feeling?*

- *What is the truth that lies beyond my justifications and excuses when I spend beyond my means?*

- *Is there an item that I genuinely believe will enrich my life, but which seems out of my reach?*

- *Am I asking for a win-win solution or settling for something less?*

A Warrior mentality will promote working hard to earn what you want while a Wise One mentality will promote working hard to become the person you must be in order to receive it.

Chapter 9
Does Your Premise Allow For Miracles?
Warrior Versus Wise One

Do you believe in miracles—changes that occur as if by magic? Or do your premises—your basic assumptions about reality—exclude their possibility?

Premises based on a *Warrior* mentality promote fighting for what you want and defending what you have. Miracles appear arbitrary. Premises based on a *Wise One* mentality promote feeling your disappointment all the way back to its roots for the purpose of learning, healing and growth. Miracles appear to logically reflect the new order.

A *Warrior* mentality promotes working hard to earn what you want while a *Wise One* mentality promotes working hard to become the person you must be in order to receive it. A Wise One knows that every day is a miracle, some just stand out more than others.

Our premises determine our responses to life; they determine our capacity to thrive physically, socially and financially. The premise we adopt is a choice even when it's an unconscious one.

When something is confusing it is always beneficial to check the premises from which we base our responses. For example, in the face of conflict do you fight (Warrior) or do you seek understanding (Wise One)? Our society tends to have a Warrior mentality: we fight for peace, we battle with our weight, we war against drugs, we tackle illness.

Can this expenditure of our energy work effectively, especially when the problem itself indicates that we are already over-expended?

Seeking Understanding versus Doing Battle

What if we were to seek understanding instead of doing battle?

What if the problems listed above are actually showing us aspects of ourselves as individuals and as a society that are ready for change?

And what if these changes could bring us our desired outcomes in a way that fighting never could?

Wise Ones know this to be true. They know that their conflicts are actually in support of their becoming more authentic in their living and loving by showing them where they are weak in these areas. They know that emerging as a victor from a physical, social or financial challenge means emerging wiser and more compassionate rather than emerging as the winner of a battle. Wise Ones know that the feelings stirred by a challenge are designed to take us back to where we need to go to make our changes—to show us why we are seeing signs of depletion—if only we would learn to respond to them rather than react to them.

When we fight a problem (Warrior) we turn it into the enemy and go on the warpath. When we see it as a messenger (Wise One), we heed its call for change and set out on the healing path.

The most fundamental premise we hold is about the nature of the world we live in. Is it friend—designed to help us—or foe—designed to hinder us?

A premise that the world is designed to help us is a premise that initiates change from the inside out rather than forcing change on the outside as a substitute for change on the inside—as a substitute for developing our mastery for living and loving.

Some old people are wise, and some are just old. The *wise* have mastered living and loving with grace while the *old* (Warriors) have mastered living and loving with force—controlling, outsmarting, debating, defending and manipulating in an effort to outwit suffering versus lifting ourselves out of suffering through learning to live and love more authentically. Living and loving with grace is living and loving in a balanced, fluid, pure, uplifting way. Living and loving with force is living in fear-of-losing-love. It is corrupted, pushy and depleting. Thus it can only serve to bring us down further and harden us.

I am not suggesting that you take no action in resolving problems, or promoting Warrior or Wise One mentalities. I am attempting to demonstrate how actions motivated by love will be different from those motivated by fear, and that the outcomes of those actions will also be different.

What Influences Our Premises?

Influences such as family, religion, society and schooling shape our premises; we interpret life based on this foundation. When we believe our world is designed to help us, we run toward it in anticipation of support, but if we believe our world is designed to hurt us we shy away from it by focusing on suffering and how to avoid it.

A premise that the world is filled with suffering calls forth from us dramatically different responses than are called forth by a world filled with support. The voices of so-called reason inside our heads tell us stories about ourselves, our circumstances and others based on these premises. I use the term 'reason' loosely because these voices are only as reasonable as the premises from which they spring forth.

Based on my premise that the world is designed to help us, I believe that our prayers are always answered, that every day is a miracle, that a miracle is a product of our desires, and that Love is the fabric from which miracles are made.

Far from wishful thinking, these beliefs have emerged from some of the deepest, darkest moments of my life. The truth did not reveal itself in the midst of my battles, but rather in the moments when I stopped fighting, and surrendered long enough to ask questions such as, "Why me?" "Why this?" "Why now?" and "Why not?" When I asked, I was always shown the answer. Over time I learned to stop wasting time fighting and to ask as my first rather than my last resort. I learned the value of seeking understanding and it opened me up to a world that could provide answers.

Have you ever gotten into a power struggle with your children over chores?

Case Study:

I frequently found myself cleaning around my husband and kids as they unwound in front of the television after dinner. It was common for me to collapse into bed at night, having missed the couch altogether. I believed that it was just easier to do things myself than to ask for help. But was it?

Twenty-or-so years ago a chronic health issue provided me with an opportunity to re-think this premise. Initially my focus was on fighting the debilitating repetitive strain injury. The kids and hubby did step up to help in my incapacitation, but after a stretch of no improvement my daughter asked, "Are we going to get paid extra allowance for doing more chores?"

I was devastated. I thought, "I have done my children a huge disservice. I haven't taught them how to give." This exchange brought awareness to my premises. I had been coming at my children as opponents—as a Warrior—in anticipation of having to battle for their help. Thus battles are what I got, except for the winning part.

No one won, even when they did concede to help because how could my heart feel good about making them feel bad?

In hindsight, I can see that taking my focus off of fighting my health issue and placing it on seeking to understand what I was unconsciously modeling for my children, why, and how I could be more supportive of us all being more loving human beings, helped with my healing process. I had been shouldering too much responsibility and debilitating neck and shoulder spasms were reflecting it. The weight of the world I chose to carry was taking its toll.

A Wise One is the leader of a team and approaches the situation respectfully, expecting support and desiring for everyone to emerge a winner.

Once I blew off the steam my failed-Warrior approach had created, forgave myself and my children, and donned a

Wise One hat, I was able to ask for what I needed, communicate why I needed it, and explain how everyone would benefit individually and collectively because of it. I became enthusiastic rather than angry, interested in how everyone felt about my requests rather than judgmental, and with help I was able to enjoy a little down time with my family in the evenings rather than irritably working around them.

Wise Ones wouldn't trade their experiences for anyone else's, not even the suffering parts, because they have all been rich with value. That doesn't mean they would choose suffering, but when it shows up, they pay attention. This Wise One mentality, as I have come to call it, continues to expand to encompass deeper Truths and greater Love. When we pursue understanding—learning, healing and growth—through our experiences, our realities will reflect the luminosity of our changes. Sometimes we have to delve deeper in order to soar higher.

Warpath Versus Healing Path

As a Wise One, we know that our world is designed in support of our pursuits and that our power lies in our capacity to be truthful and loving—the more truthful and loving, the more powerful we become and the more powerful we are, the more luminous our lives become.

Every day is a miracle: Fight and the universe will bring

us opponents. Seek understanding and the universe will bring us partners.

Health, relationship and financial problems serve to signal a need for development—they are calls to change an aspect of how we live and love—an indication of imbalance—either too much energy is going out or our energy is stagnant. When on the warpath, we are fighting our messengers and resisting the very changes that can bring us back into balance.

"Insanity: doing the same thing over and over again and expecting different results." ~ Albert Einstein[6]

Let's apply Einstein's definition of insanity here and stop using the very force that caused our problems in expectation that it would alleviate them. When we seek understanding, in the faith that a *problem* is actually a call to mature from Warrior to Wise One —a call to purify and balance our loving—changes logically occur as they did in my own warrior to wise one example.

We can be Warrior in one area of our life and Wise One in another and a junior Wise One in yet another since development in different aspects of our lives occurs at different rates. When we are on the warpath—applying force—it's a sign that we are resisting feeling some suffering that is already present inside ourselves and we are fighting its reflection outside ourselves. This approach can only serve to spread suffering by causing harm to others and/or by causing additional suffering to ourselves. When on the warpath in my example, I was demonstrating this very harm—my children weren't learning to be a part of a team and I was carrying the burden until it broke me. It's not about choosing our battles, it's about stepping off of the combat position.

A Warrior believes that his fear is a weakness and will repress it (which takes force and is thus depleting) in his effort to be strong. But a Wise One is honest with himself when he is fearful because he knows that is the loving thing to do—he knows how truth and love work to his advantage when they are pure (free of fear) and balanced. This wisdom, when applied, is his strength.

How The Wise One Handles The Warrior

The Wise One has not dismissed the inner Warrior but has stopped giving it decision-making authority. He acknowledges his humanness, so when he catches himself applying force, perhaps by pushing for someone else to change, he knows it is a heads-up that he has met resistance to feeling suffering inside himself.

A Warrior will push for the other person to change so that he won't have to feel the feelings the other person's behavior is stirring in him. (The other person has his/her own set of issues but is also a messenger.) From here the Wise One will us his *Warrior* energy toward seeking and tending to his suffering—in search of understanding rather than trying to change others. In the end a Wise One may invite others to change with her, but she is changing regardless.

In Conclusion

- The premise that the world is designed to help us does not require for us to seek growth.

- Reaching our highest potential will neither preclude nor protect us from suffering.

- The power to experience a luminously miraculous existence is in our hands.

- Suffering is not what we think it is and fighting it just causes it to spread.

- How we receive our lives is our choice.

"Seek and ye shall find." ~ (Matthew 7:7 King James Version) If we are looking for a fight, we will find one and if we are looking to reach our highest potential, we will be provided with everything we need to do so. Our prayers are always answered though sometimes we don't realize what we have been praying for until it is standing there in front of us. Transitioning from Warrior to Wise One takes more than a flip-of-a-switch, but the efforts are far-reaching. It can take a dark moment for us to wake up to a deeper truth and seek a better way, but those who have, look back with gratitude.

Our lives are designed to help us be as honest and loving as we desire—sometimes by showing us where we are not being so loving or honest or by being on the receiving end of a similar ignorance—in other words, by bringing us physical, social or financial "problems" to expose our premises.

"There is no such thing as a problem without a gift for you in its hands. You seek problems because you need their gifts." ~ Richard Bach[7]

Based on a Wise One premise life is very orderly—people don't just randomly show up in our lives and situations don't just indiscriminately occur. Our life is all being orchestrated by our energy while simultaneously being divinely orchestrated—everyone is getting what they need to fulfill their premise at the same time as you are and that is pretty miraculous.

Why me? Why now? Why not?

Questions for disclosing your premise:

- *What is the premise of my family? Religion?*

- *Is it easier to do things myself or to ask for help?*

- *In the face of conflict do I fight or seek understanding?*

- *Do I run toward life or shy away from it?*

- *Do I try to change others or accept them where*

they stand?

Real strength is born of humility—having the courage to admit when I am bothered and knowing how to use my feelings to lighten my past, illuminate my present, and brighten my future.

Chapter 10
Why Can't I Just Get Over It?

Finding a new dentist had been on my to-do-list since before my last checkup. But there on my answering machine was a new message—you guessed it—confirming my next cleaning.

Have you ever been meaning to do something yet find yourself putting it off?

Or have you had a project that kept getting carried forward from one to-do-list to the next?

I called and cancelled my appointment. At least it was one step in the right direction. But three months later I still hadn't had my semi-annual checkup. I'd gone every six months for practically my entire life. I almost just gave in and made an appointment with the old dentist, but something in me was ready to move forward so I called a hygienist friend instead. I told her what I was looking for in a dentist, she handed me over to their receptionist, and the appointment was made.

Phew!! A sense of euphoria came over me the instant the

phone hit the cradle.

How do you feel when you finish a project that has been hanging over your head? Relieved? Lighter? Energized?

That is because you are no longer feeding it your energy. Even when not consciously thinking about an unfinished project there is an undercurrent of energy necessary to keep it alive. Finishing the project frees up that energy.

Why did it take me so long to complete that last liberating step?

As Trish Whynot, my inquisitive mind wants to know. I want to go after the buried treasure because my findings never fail to add richness to my life. My intuition tells me that understanding why it took me so long to find a new dentist will be fruitful.

You might be rolling your eyes about now, thinking, "It's just a dentist, Trish." *But is it? Just a dentist* would not have caused me to procrastinate, especially when my friend is a hygienist.

Has anyone ever told you some version of, "just get over it" when you've been struggling?

Or encouraged you to let go of an experience before you were ready?

Did you feel shame for being accused of making too big a

deal out of it?

Maybe it seemed to others that you were making a big deal out of whatever it was because they didn't know the whole story. So let me share more of my story.

I had the greatest dentist in the world. Not only was he a great dentist, but he had been my dentist since childhood. He acknowledged my whole person, not just my mouth.

I loved my dentist's fatherly nature. When my children were young, he'd take extra time after my appointment to let them lie back in the chair while he counted their teeth. It only took a moment, showed how much he cared, and built trust between them. When they were old enough for cleanings, we all reaped the rewards. I never had to battle with them over a dental visit; they felt relaxed and safe with him, and so did I. But then he retired and left us in the hands of a dentist who I really didn't care for.

Has anyone who touched you deeply ever moved on from your life or been lifted out of it before you were ready to let them go?

A death, a divorce, a loved one moving?

How did you feel?

My feelings were:

- sadness because I was grieving. Although I was

happy for him I was sad for me because I was experiencing loss.

- abandonment because he moved on and left me with this other dentist.

- anger because I wasn't ready to let him go. He even gave us a good year's notice, but are we ever ready to let go of someone we cherish?

- regret because I didn't realize how he had touched my heart until it was too late to let him know.

Now, you might be rolling your eyes again. "Come on, Trish, abandoned by a dentist?" "Grieving?" "Touched your heart?" *Isn't that a bit much?*

Initially I thought my anger came from my frustration with the dentist I had been left with, but it took my moving on from her to realize that she hadn't been as bad as I had been telling myself. What my frustration had truly been telling me was that I had not been ready to let go of my beloved childhood dentist. As a rule, when strong feelings are triggered —especially if those feelings seem out of proportion to the situation at hand—it is a signal that they connect to something else in our past, something we haven't dealt with. Therefore, I figured that once I began my grieving process that other experiences of *letting go* would be tied in.

To understand this, let's think about rhizomes. A mint

plant spreads not only by producing seeds, but by sending out underground runners called rhizomes. The rhizome then produces roots and sprouts that develop into a new plant, which sends out another rhizome, which sprouts another plant, and so on. Our life experiences are connected to each other much like the mint plants are connected by these rhizomes. I had experienced a string of losses, all of which were connected by this underground system. The rhizomes of mint are shallow (but tough), so when you pull on one plant it causes a chain reaction—which disturbs the other plants, much like my feelings of loss.

As I put two and two together, my procrastination and my excessive frustration with my retiring dentist's replacement, it became obvious that I was experiencing loss, and that it was bigger than just my dentist. From there I used my feelings of abandonment as fuel to go into the rhizomes of my past—the conduit for my energy that was still feeding some partially grieved losses. I landed at another physical manifestation of loss—a painful breakup from my teen years. It was traumatic for many reasons and my pride—my old version of strength, which was to pretend that I wasn't bothered—along with my lack of emotional maturity, prevented me from processing it at the time. It took me years to get over that, but had I truly gotten over it or had the memory just become distant with time?

Now again, you might be thinking, "Come on, Trish, don't

you have more important things to do than rehash something that happened more than 30 years ago?"

Over the course of my adult years I have come to know that real strength is born of humility—having the courage to admit when I am bothered and knowing how to use my feelings to lighten my past, illuminate my present, and brighten my future. Based on this understanding, I knew with certainty that this was *the most important thing to do right now*. I realized that the feelings I had around my dentist retiring had forced old feelings of loss to the surface; I had disturbed the underground rhizome system, so that I could suddenly see and feel the interconnectedness of these experiences.

Instead of smoothing over the disturbed soil, I dug in. And just as expected, I emerged from this visit into my past with some pearls—the value I had lost from believing that I had been discarded and the wisdom of knowing, without a doubt, that I had not been the victim I once thought I had been. These findings were hugely liberating for me.

Rather than seeing myself as jilted, I now saw the loss of that relationship as part of the natural process of growth and change. As part of this natural process, a restructuring takes place where some people fall out of our lives and we fall out of theirs because we have moved out of alignment in some way.

That's what had happened with my dentist. He no longer wanted to be a dentist and I still needed one. Our journeys had simply gone in separate directions. All of a sudden I could clearly see that this was also what had happened with this boyfriend and with other losses in my past. Our desires for our futures were too different; our paths had crossed but then had to diverge. But at the time all I could do was blame and become the victim.

With this realization, along with the work I had done leading up to it, I was able to put closure to an entire string of similar events, which freed up even more energy. I went into this conduit believing I had been a victim of abandonment and emerged knowing I, and the people around me, had simply changed and that those who reflected our changes (some new, some old) would naturally gather around us. Knowledge is not meant to diminish the hurt we experience, but through having the humility to feel our hurt we are able to embody our knowledge with every fiber of our being rather than holding it only as head knowledge.

Rather than add another event to my string of losses, looking deeper into my procrastination had brought closure to many of the events on the string, liberated my energy, and revealed wisdom that was invaluable to my future. My string of losses had morphed into a string of pearls that I could thrive on.

From the closure of these old abandonments had emerged an entirely new, lighter and more hopeful dimension to *letting go*. My future holds the promise that rather than being emotionally charged by a string of past events, *letting go* will become an occasion for gratitude: I will still grieve the loss over what will no longer be, but I'll be able to be grateful for what was, and expect something at least as good, if not better—something that matches the new me—to be just around the corner. I'll also be expecting that everyone involved will be getting exactly what they need at the same time, just as I have.

Why did it take me so long to complete that last liberating step?

Because I had been subconsciously struggling with *it's just a dentist, I am a victim* and *there's nothing better out there*. I was viewing my present, and my desires for my future through the filters of my past. I may have to test drive a few dentists before I find a good fit, but I know without a doubt that it will be worth the effort in more ways than I can currently wrap my mind around.

Next time you are told (or want to tell someone) to *just get over it*, think about the string of pearls that came from my dentist story. There may be some buried treasure underfoot for you as well, if you accept your invitation to potentially lighten your past, illuminate your present and positively change the course of your future.

Why me? Why now? Why not?

When an event triggers more emotion than a situation should warrant:

- *Feel the feelings around it.*

- *See if any memories bubble up from times you have felt this way before.*

- *Respond to those emotions fully and look for the deeper meanings and opportunities they present.*

- *Then look at the current situation again.*

- *It will likely look different and you will likely address it differently.*

- *If you react to the current situation first it is recommended that you go back to the emotional components afterwards. In hindsight, how would you have addressed it differently?*

Pets become a part of who we are and how we love. In this way they will always be with us.

Chapter 11
Who's Tickling My Face?
Steps For Grieving The Loss Of A Pet

When I went into the dining area to fill Steve's bowl and found his food from the night before untouched again, my heart sank. Our seventeen-year-old orange tabby had been losing his spunk over the past year. My inkling was that he was preparing to leave us but with the kids home on summer break I found myself holding onto the hope that they had fed him and that my rejected offerings had been seconds.

Preliminary Grieving

As a counselor I know the importance of carving out time for grieving so along with giving Steve an appetite stimulant prescribed by the vet, I took some time off to be with my feelings. They fluctuated from sadness to fear to anger to regret. I gave myself permission to feel them all.

My sadness was at the thought of missing Steve's loving, to which I had become accustomed. If you were looking for Steve at night, you would often find him at the foot of the bed of whoever needed a little extra love. This potential loss of affection also stirred up feelings from other losses of unconditional love that I had yet to grieve, so I took the time to grieve those too.

My fear was the fear of not knowing what Steve's final days would bring or how they would play out. Would he die peacefully in his sleep? Would he wander off to die—leaving us to wonder what happened? Or would I be faced with the decision to euthanize?

My anger was about Steve leaving the planet before I was ready for him to go. I was completely myself with Steve because he accepted all of me—even those parts of me that I hid from others for fear of judgment. I had been meaning to love those insecure parts that Steve had so effortlessly shown me how to love, but now these parts were standing impatiently before me. I could either attempt to continue pacifying them with a new cat, shut myself off from these fragile parts of me or do my inner work and love them myself.

My regret was for the times I had pushed Steve's love aside—taken it for granted. When I would walk through the door with groceries, he would greet me in the hallway, rub up against my legs and purr contentedly. But with a job and three children I was often thinking about what to cook for dinner rather than about fully receiving Steve's greeting and returning the affection. I was also feeling regret over the irrational "what-ifs?" What if I had done this or that differently? Would Steve have lost his will to live if I had been a better guardian? Would we be dealing with this if I had listened to my first inkling and brought him to the vet sooner?

This was my first opportunity to put my most mature understanding of grief into practice and it was proving to be ripe with opportunities for learning, healing and growth. The more healing I did, the more love and appreciation I had, and the more present I could be with Steve during his final days.

Feelings Of Loss

Steve's greatest gift in life was his modeling of unconditional love; and his greatest gift in death was in showing me where and how to apply what he had modeled. His loss not only revealed pain from other un-grieved and semi-grieved losses but also from desires for unconditional love that I had abandoned during childhood. There's always that someone in our lives who 'loves' us as they see fit rather than as we desire. Because we feel that we need their love, we abandon our desire. My history of loss had caused me to lean a little harder on Steve's love, which consequently had intensified the pain I experienced from losing him. This was valuable information—not for the purpose of blaming, but for the purpose of healing and growth. Perhaps those who loved me *as they had seen fit* had been leaning a little too hard on me in their own way? This awareness was a key component for completing the forgiveness process, and liberating me from my past.

The intensity of emotional pain can be confusing, surprising and even embarrassing when we don't understand it. Fear that others will be insensitive to the magnitude of emotion we are experiencing may motivate us to bury our pain or to keep busy to avoid it, but these efforts only serve to prolong our discomfort and deter us from our gifts.

Being loved *as-is*, is a desire which every human being has. Therefore, our fear of losing our pet's unconditional love can cloud our ability to make decisions that are in the best interest of the animal. Fortunately Steve was patient with our process and didn't seem to take it personally. Although my grieving had helped me to separate my needs from Steve's, our vet was there to offer facts and gentle guidance in our confusion during those final days.

The Choice To Euthanize

As a pet's guardian, putting a pet down is likely to be within the realm of decisions we have to make. This can be difficult when a pet holds family-member status. My desire was to be respectful of where our responsibility as Steve's guardian ended and his responsibility for his destiny began. Sometimes all I could do was hold the intention when the boundary was unclear, and trust it to guide me in the right direction.

Steve did not die from an illness. We had hoped that his choice to stop eating had been due to a heat wave. When tests from the vet proved inconclusive she suggested we try an appetite stimulant. This got him eating but each time we stopped the stimulant, it was only a matter of days before the cycle would begin again.

Prior to the last attempt with the appetite stimulant, our family made peace with Steve—each member said goodbye in their own way.

In our goodbyes we touched on:

- our love for Steve.

- shared memories.

- what we were grateful for about him.

- apologies for things we wished we had done differently.

- thanks for his patience with us.

- our respect for his choice to either stick around for a while longer or to move on.

One may argue that Steve didn't understand a word we said. But a pet feels the love, sincerity and gratitude conveyed through the heartfelt tone of our voice as we speak the words. By making peace we were no longer holding Steve here and I do believe that that felt better for all of us.

Steve had simply lost his zest for life. Weak, thin and withdrawn from weeks of on-again-off-again eating, he made his decision clear and we prepared to honor it. Euthanization seemed best since, had it not been for our intervention, he would have already passed. Steve had been patient with our process of letting go and for that we were grateful.

On that last trip to the vet my emotions fluctuated from sadness for our impending loss, to doubting our choice to euthanize, to a sense of peace for being able to genuinely honor Steve's choice. The vet was reassuring. She allowed us time and privacy for our final goodbyes. Steve was given a sedative while laying peacefully in our arms and euthanized with her loving assistance.

The Message

On our way home we stopped by a wildlife sanctuary to be close to nature. As we walked along the meandering path I kept noticing a tickle on the side of my face as though my hair was brushing against it. But each time I reached over to brush the hair away, there was nothing there. I silently acknowledged my confusion and the connection I made was that every time I had thought about Steve or spoken his name it was followed by this sensation. The message I kept getting was: *He is now free to be with you always*. I didn't understand what that truly meant for days, even years, to come.

I had done my preliminary grieving, but my tears were telling me that there was more to do. Steve's passing revealed more of what we loved about him and of how he had shared his love for us. When I opened a can of tuna there was no one to come out of the woodwork—no one to rub up against my legs until he got his serving of the juice in a saucer. There was no one to stop and pet on the couch, no one to call home at night before going to sleep. But at least it was easier to welcome this next bout of feelings because of all the healing that had emerged from my earlier experience. My feelings were messengers guiding me into places inside myself that were ready for cleansing and expansion.

I have learned the value of making time to love whoever inside of me is grieving in the unconditional way that Steve loved me. I live more, love more and am more in part because of Steve. I am not sure how else he might be with me today, but in this way I am certain he will always be with me.

New Pet or No Pet

In losing Steve I had also lost that safe environment in which it felt great to be myself. When he was asleep on the couch it provided me with an excuse to slow down and join him for a petting or two. He had this loud purr that was activated by any family member's presence in his general vicinity. When we'd pull into the driveway he'd appear out of seemingly nowhere and saunter over to the front door to join us.

Although tempting, I knew that getting another animal to fill my void would only provide temporary relief at best. I didn't want to burden a new pet or step up my feelings of dependency or fear-of-loss. I intuitively knew that learning to delight in myself as Steve had was the only way for me to truly and permanently be myself again.

In utilizing my grief as an opportunity for learning, healing and growth I could see how Steve had gradually brought me out of my shell over the years. I could be tired, loving, frustrated, broke, and yet still be equally delightful to Steve.

As I resolved the issues that had surfaced through Steve's loss I realized that I could adopt another pet for the pure reverence of it, or choose to experience my newfound freedom of feeling more whole in other ways.

Down the road we did opt for another pet. Because of what we had learned from our time with Steve our next experience offered a much deeper, more enriching, delightful and mutually supportive experience.

In Conclusion

Our interactions with our pets provide us with a wealth of information about ourselves in relation to love including our resistances to it. The more we make peace with the source of our resistances through grieving loss, the less dependent we will be on another animal (or human) to feel complete. We can adopt another pet if we wish or enjoy our newfound freedom, but either choice will be simply for the pleasure and expansion of love.

The contrast of having Steve in my life and then removed reminded me of where I had closed off to being myself with others and of how great it feels to open up again. Grieving was the process that helped me to remain open. My ability to connect, even with our two new kitties, is a reflection of my reconnection with myself. Steve has become a part of who I am and how I love and for that I am eternally grateful.

Experiencing my grief as an opportunity for soul searching—self-exploration, self-evaluation and self-expansion—filled me with more love and gratitude for Steve and others from my past, as well as greater compassion for myself and for humanity. Steve left me with the gift of reconnection with myself.

Why me? Why now? Why not?

Questions for beginning the process of reconnection:

- *What do I miss that my pet provided? (affection, companionship, unconditional love, a sense of value)*

- *How did I receive my pet's love? (welcome it, put it off, dismiss it)*

- *How did I express my love for my pet? (with play, with treats, with snuggling, with care)*

- *Was my care for my pet consistent with my care for myself?*

- *Where was it easy to be myself with my pet but difficult to be as authentic with people?*

Don't do what you do to please someone or in hopes of a particular outcome. Do it because it makes you smile with contentment for the person you are at the end of the day.

Chapter 12
What's In a Smile?

It is morning. I am sitting on our deck—warm air soothing my skin, blue skies making way for the dappling of sunlight, and local songbirds leading the morning's concerto. I'm in my pj's, sipping coffee, plans only to have no plans.

Every fiber of my being is smiling with contentment this Sunday morning. Immersed in comfort; nothing is pressing, nothing is tugging, and the elements surrounding me depict the epitome of my personal definition of magnificence.

I desire to be touched by it all: the sights, the sounds, the smells, the tastes, the sensations. I breathe in every morsel, welcoming each to permeate my very being. My smile is an outward acknowledgment of my gratitude for being quenched with pleasure.

I was smiling from the inside out this glorious morning, but it hasn't always been this way.

I was never officially diagnosed as Type A, but twenty-five

years ago—when I tore through life at an alarmingly overachieving pace—I guarantee you, I could not have found joy in this moment.

Yoga was too slow.

I grew vegetables because I couldn't see the value of a flower garden.

And I walked through life with more important things to do than immerse myself in my surroundings. Or so I thought.

Health issues prompted me to disengage from that 60mph approval-seeking hamster wheel where stress was clenched between my teeth, coursing through my veins and oozing out my sinuses. When my tightly wound Type A muscles began tweaking—cutting off nerves and sensation, much as I had cut myself off from what curls the corners of my mouth—life as I knew it came to a screeching halt. In hindsight, "Thank God!"

A Genuine Smile

"A smile is the light in the window of your face that tells people you're at home." ~ Author Unknown[8]

A genuine smile requires a willingness to be vulnerable. It reveals the pleasure that quenches our hearts and souls. A smile exposes our individuality. It is our truest expression of contentment—acknowledgment that our hunger has been satisfied.

What brings a smile to my face may not be what brings a smile to yours; but if you are comfortable with your smile, you will delight in mine. This is how smiles spread.

Feeling Safe To Share

I was not afraid to let Nature know how deeply She touched me that glorious Sunday morning, nor am I afraid to share it with you now. But it hasn't always been that way either. Those we feel free to genuinely smile around are those we feel safe to share our deepest selves with.

Sharing this sacred moment with you puts me at risk of your judgment, as does a genuine smile. If I were seeking your approval I would fear loss, but since I seek to inspire us both, I see only gain for both of us.

A genuine smile is not dependent on someone else's response; it is merely an acknowledgment of what is. If we allow ourselves to become attached to the opinions of others, then so too will our smiles become dependent on outside approval. Getting untangled from this form of codependency may require tweezers and a magnifying glass, but it is totally doable and worth the effort.

Our genuine smile will weed out anyone who is not supportive of us being our authentic selves, while the light it provides serves as a beacon for those who are. However, fear of this weeding can be the very reason many people withhold or even abandon their smiles.

The Approval Smile

"The reward for conformity is that everyone likes you but yourself." ~ Rita Mae Brown[9]

I lost my smile and consequently myself, as many do, in my efforts to conform to religious beliefs, societal standards and family ideals that were well intended but negatively impactful. I had learned to be who others wanted me to be at the expense of being myself. This behavior is deceitful, exhausting and lacks integrity, but living on autopilot, I was unaware of its impact both internally and externally.

In my approval-seeking days, my smile was dependent on external praise. I tried to be who my friends wanted me to be in order to be accepted, who my kids wanted me to be in order to be loved, who my boss wanted me to be in order to be appreciated—I thought that was what love called for.

External praise has kind of a caffeine effect. It lifts us up temporarily but when the boost wears off it leaves us seeking our next boost. That is why the hamster wheel gets so crazy— it leaves us incessantly at the heels of a smile. As caffeine can be a temporary antidote for sleep deprivation, approval can be a temporary antidote for fulfillment deprivation. But in the end both leave us dependent on the antidote rather than satiated and smiling.

Those whose autopilot is approval, like mine used to be, often give 150% at work and/or in relationships in their attempts to fill the shoes of expectation laid out for them by others or by themselves. Super-efforts that leave us feeling drained, underappreciated and with a smile dependent on someone else's satisfaction will eventually wear us down and tear us apart.

Sometimes it takes physical, financial or relationship collapse to bring us back to our proverbial drawing boards— to what we were taught or how we interpreted it on a foundational level. When we live attached to the opinions of others we lose ourselves, and it can take tweezers and a magnifying glass to separate out where our generosity should end and their responsibility should begin.

Learning from Mistakes

"Mistakes are part of the dues one pays for a full life." ~ Sophia Loren[10]

Mistakes are part of giving life our best shot. Sometimes we don't know what needs fine-tuning, tweaking or changing completely in ourselves until our outer world collapses— taking our smile down with it—as a reflection of our inner discord.

Case Study:

Aaron came to me with financial struggles. He thought

more money would bring a smile to his face but his business decisions kept coming up dry. In the end, admitting to his fear of confronting his marriage partner's insistence on spending beyond their means was what steered him away from bankruptcy.

It wasn't about the money; resolution of the financial issue rested on revealing his inability to build anything deep and meaningful with his partner on the foundation of a spending disagreement. Aaron had been taught to compromise to keep the peace and he had unwittingly compromised his own integrity. Following some soul searching, Aaron and his partner came to an agreement they both felt good about (both smiling) and the money came flowing in.

Aaron and I each had our own autopilots for smiling in agreement on the outside while frowning in disagreement on the inside. This is stressful behavior—codependent and born from a foundation of fear-of-loss rather than an insistence on love. Compromising who we are (being who someone else wants us to be) and/or abandoning what we believe with our whole hearts to be best, are acts lacking in integrity. We can't claim integrity as a virtue when we change who we are and what we believe every time we fear loss.

Might you have your own version of this autopilot?

In Conclusion

"A smile is the lighting system of the face, the cooling system of the head and the heating system of the heart." ~ Author Unknown[11]

A genuine smile indicates when we are at home with who we are and with what we do. When immersed in surroundings where all the elements are pleasing to our senses and we feel safe letting it be known, is when we cast forth our greatest genuine smiles. Such heart and soul quenching activities are energizing, illuminating and rejuvenating. When an activity supports being at home with ourselves, and being at home with ourselves supports an activity, it's a good hamster wheel—filling us up instead of tearing us down.

Clients often find their way to my office when lack of return on their approval-seeking efforts reaches a collapse point such as Aaron's. Collapses can appear on the surface as physical, relationship or financial in nature, but as you can see from Aaron's and my situations, restoration includes a smile adjustment.

Approval is great as the frosting on the cake, but as the cake itself, it will eventually harden, leaving us feeling like anything but smiling. Every now and then, I still experience my own collapses, have to get out my tweezers and magnifying glass, and make my way back to the drawing board to review my autopilots, just like everyone else. But it's not so intimidating now because I know how to use it all to better direct my energy toward creating autopilots that support more genuine smiling and consequently, their spread.

Why me? Why now? Why not?

Recipe for a life filled with genuine smiles:

- *Don't do what you do to please someone or in hopes of a particular outcome.*

- *Do it because it makes you smile with contentment for the person you are at the end of the day.*

- *Give life your best shot, keep fine-tuning, tweaking, changing and emerging with grander and grander smiles.*

Endnotes

[1] Brainyquote.com, Xplore Inc, 2012. Accessed August 30, 2012.
http://www.brainyquote.com/quotes/quotes/a/alberteins148778.html

[2] White, Ellen G. 2002. The Desire of Ages. Nampa, Idaho: Pacific Press Publishing Association, 22.

[3] Bach, Richard. 1977. Illusions: The Adventures of a Reluctant Messiah. London: Random House, Ltd., 110.

[4] Scripture taken from the New King James Version®. Copyright © 1982 by Thomas Nelson, Inc. Used by permission. All rights reserved.

[5] Scripture taken from the New King James Version®. Copyright © 1982 by Thomas Nelson, Inc. Used by permission. All rights reserved.

[6] Brainyquote.com, Xplore Inc, 2012. Accessed August 23, 2012.
http://www.brainyquote.com/quotes/quotes/a/alberteins133991.html

[7] Bach, Richard. 1977. Illusions: The Adventures of a Reluctant Messiah. London: Random House, Ltd., 57.

[8] About.com Quotations. Accessed August 30, 2012.
http://quotations.about.com/od/funnyquotes/a/smile.htm

[9] BrainyQuote.com, Xplore Inc, 2012. Accessed July 31, 2012.
http://www.brainyquote.com/quotes/quotes/r/ritamaebro383520.html

[10] BrainyQuote.com, Xplore Inc, 2012. Accessed August 30, 2012.
http://www.brainyquote.com/quotes/quotes/s/sophialore106786.html

[11] ThinkExist.com, 2012. Accessed August 30, 2012.
http://thinkexist.com/quotation/a_smile_is_the_lighting_system_of_the_face-the/289357.html

CPSIA information can be obtained at www.ICGtesting.com
Printed in the USA
BVOW08s2215180814

363360BV00011B/158/P